Laughing Around The Globe: 130 Geography Jokes.

Gabriel Mensah

DEDICATION

To all the pun lovers out there, who find joy in wordplay and laughter in every corner of life. This book is for you.

To my family and friends, whose humor and love light up my world. Your endless support and laughter inspire every page.

And to the reader, may these puns bring a smile to your face and a chuckle to your heart. Thank you for sharing this pun-tastic journey with me.

Table of Contents

ACKNOWLEDGMENTS

Creating this book has been a journey filled with laughter, creativity, and collaboration. I am deeply grateful to everyone who contributed their wit and wisdom to bring this pun-tastic collection to life.

First and foremost, I want to thank my amazing family and friends for their endless support and encouragement. Your sense of humor and playful spirit inspired many of the jokes found within these pages.

To my fellow pun enthusiasts, thank you for sharing your favorite puns and jokes, sparking countless ideas, and keeping the creative juices flowing. Your love for wordplay and laughter is what makes this book truly special.

A heartfelt thank you to my editor and publisher, whose keen eyes and attention to detail ensured that every joke landed with precision and clarity. Your guidance and expertise have been invaluable.

Lastly, to you, the reader, thank you for embarking on this humorous journey with me. Your laughter and enjoyment are what makes all the effort worthwhile. I hope this book brings as much joy to your heart as it brought to mine while creating it.

Here's to many more moments of laughter and shared smiles. Happy reading!

CHAPTER 1: ANIMAL ANTICS

Welcome to the wild world of Animal Antics! In this chapter, we've gathered 130 puns that will make you chuckle, groan, and share with your friends. Enjoy the animal kingdom like never before with these clever and corny jokes.

1. Why don't fish play basketball? Because they're afraid of the net!

2. What do you call an alligator in a vest? An investigator!

3. How do you fit more pigs on your farm? Build a sty-scraper!

4. What's a cat's favorite color? Purrr-ple!

5. Why did the elephant sit on the marshmallow? To keep from falling into the hot chocolate!

6. How do bees brush their hair? With honeycombs!

7. What do you get if you cross a snake with a tasty dessert? A pie-thon!

8. Why are cats bad storytellers? They only have one tail!

9. What do you call a sleeping bull? A bulldozer!

10. What do you get from a pampered cow? Spoiled milk!

11. Why do fish always know how much they weigh? They have their own scales!

12. Why did the scarecrow win an award? He was outstanding in his field!

13. What's black and white and red all over? A sunburnt penguin!

14. Why don't seagulls fly over the bay? Because then they'd be bagels!

15. How do you catch a squirrel? Climb a tree and act like a nut!

16. Why did the cow go to space? To see the moooon!

17. What do you call a bear with no teeth? A gummy bear!

18. Why do chickens sit on eggs? Because they don't have chairs!

19. Why was the horse so happy? Because it lived in a stable environment!

20. What do you call an owl who does magic tricks? Hoo-dini!

21. Why don't bats live alone? Because they like hanging out with their friends!

22. What did the duck say when it bought lipstick? Put it on my bill!

23. How do cows stay up to date with current events? They read the moos-paper!

24. What do you get when you cross a sheep and a kangaroo? A woolly jumper!

25. Why are frogs so happy? They eat whatever bugs them!

26. Why did the crab never share? Because it's shellfish!

27. Why don't ants get sick? They have tiny ant-bodies!

28. What do you call a group of musical whales? An orca-stra!

29. How does a penguin build its house? Igloos it together!

30. Why do dolphins swim in saltwater? Because pepper makes them sneeze!

31. What do you get when you cross a snowman and a vampire? Frostbite!

32. What do you call a rabbit with fleas? Bugs Bunny!

33. How do birds stay in touch? They send tweets!

34. Why did the duck go to jail? Because it was selling quack!

35. What do you call a pig that knows karate? A pork chop!

36. Why are fish so smart? Because they live in schools!

37. What do you call a cow that can play the guitar? A moo-sician!

38. Why do gorillas have big nostrils? Because they have big fingers!

39. What's a dog's favorite city? New Yorkie!

40. Why was the baby strawberry crying? Because its parents were in a jam!

41. What do you get when you cross a sheep and a bee? A bah-humbug!

42. Why are snails bad at racing? Because they're always a bit sluggish!

43. What's a cat's favorite book? The Great Catsby!

44. How do cows do math? They use a cow-culator!

45. Why don't crabs donate to charity? Because they're shellfish!

46. What do you call a bear caught in the rain? A drizzly bear!

47. Why are spiders such know-it-alls? They're always on the web!

48. How do elephants talk to each other? They use their trunks!

49. Why do bees hum? Because they don't know the words!

50. Why did the lion eat the tightrope walker? It wanted a well-balanced meal!

51. What's a cat's favorite dessert? Mice cream!

52. Why did the koala get the job? Because it was over-koala-fied!

53. How do you make a tissue dance? Put a little boogey in it!

54. Why did the dog sit in the shade? Because it didn't want to be a hot dog!

55. What do you get if you cross a fish and an elephant? Swimming trunks!

56. Why was the sheep mad at the computer? Because it said it had too many rams!

57. How does a lion greet the other animals? "Pleased to eat you!"

58. What do you call a dancing sheep? A baa-llerina!

59. Why are cats great singers? Because they're very purr-sistent!

60. What do you call an illegally parked frog? Toad!

61. Why don't snakes drink coffee? Because it makes them viper-active!

62. How do monkeys get down the stairs? They slide down the banana-ster!

63. What do you get when you cross a snake and a pie? A pie-thon!

64. Why do ducks never grow up? They always stay little quackers!

65. What's a cow's favorite musical note? Beef-flat!

66. How do fish send messages? They drop a line!

67. Why did the crab cross the road? To get to the other tide!

68. How do turtles communicate? With shell phones!

69. Why was the rabbit so good at math? Because it could multiply!

70. Why don't alligators play cards? Because they're all cheaters!

71. What's a frog's favorite candy? Lollihops!

72. Why do birds fly south for the winter? Because it's faster than walking!

73. How do you get a squirrel to like you? Act like a nut!

74. Why was the owl so good at keeping secrets? Because it always gives a hoot!

75. What do you call a rabbit who tells jokes? A funny bunny!

76. Why don't elephants use computers? Because they're afraid of the mouse!

77. What's a horse's favorite sport? Stable tennis!

78. Why did the spider go on the computer? To check its website!

79. How do you know a dog is a great musician? It has perfect pitch!

80. What's a fish's favorite instrument? The bass guitar!

81. Why did the frog take the bus to work? His car got toad!

82. Why do cows wear bells? Because their horns don't work!

83. How do sheep stay warm in the winter? With woolly sweaters!

84. Why are giraffes so slow to apologize? It takes them a long time to swallow their pride!

85. What do you get when you cross a bird and a car? A flying vulture!

86. Why did the chicken join a band? Because it had the drumsticks!

87. How do dolphins make decisions? They flipper coin!

88. What's a cat's favorite movie? The Sound of Mewsic!

89. How do cows go on vacation? They take a moo-trip!

90. Why did the bird fly into the library? It was looking for bookworms!

91. What do you call a bear that's stuck in the rain? A drizzly bear!

92. Why don't chickens play sports? Because they're afraid of fowl play!

93. What do you call a fish with no eyes? Fsh!

94. Why do kangaroos hate rainy days? Their kids have to play inside!

95. What's a squirrel's favorite way to watch TV? With nut-flix!

96. Why do cows have hooves instead of feet? Because they lactose!

97. How do you make a goldfish age? Take away its scales!

98. Why are bats so good at baseball? They're great at catching flies!

99. What do you call a dog magician? A labracadabrador!

100. Why was the cat sitting on the computer? To keep an eye on the mouse!

101. How do you get a cow to be quiet? Press the moo-te button!

102. Why don't owls have girlfriends? Because they're a hoot alone!

103. What do you call an elephant at the North Pole? Lost!

104. How does a spider fix a broken web? With a website!

105. Why don't pigs play basketball? They might hog the ball!

106. What do you call a fish with no eyes? Fsh!

107. Why was the turtle a great comedian? He had a shell of a sense of humor!

108. What do you call an owl that does magic tricks? Hoo-dini!

109. How does a cat like its steak? Rare, like its patience!

110. What did the buffalo say to his son when he left for school? Bison!

111. Why don't chickens tell secrets? Because they might crack up!

112. How do you find Will Smith in the snow? Look for fresh prints!

113. Why do elephants never use computers? They're afraid of the mouse!

114. What's a horse's favorite sport? Stable tennis!

115. What did the frog do when his car broke down? He got it toad away!

116. Why do cows wear bells? Because their horns don't work!

117. What do you get when you cross a sheep and a kangaroo? A woolly jumper!

118. Why are giraffes so good at high jump? They never miss the mark!

119. What do you call a cow with no legs? Ground beef!

120. Why did the lion eat the tightrope walker? He wanted a well-balanced meal!

121. How do you organize a space party? You planet!

122. Why are cats bad storytellers? They only have one tale!

123. What do you call a lazy kangaroo? A pouch potato!

124. Why did the crab never share? Because he was shellfish!

125. Why don't alligators like fast food? They can't catch it!

126. How do octopuses go into battle? Well-armed!

127. Why don't ants get sick? They have tiny ant-bodies!

128. What's a cow's favorite place to hang out? The moo-seum!

129. Why do fish always sing off-key? They can't tuna fish!

130. What's a dog's favorite city? New Yorkie!

CHAPTER 2: FOOD FUNNIES

Welcome to the tasty world of Food Funnies! This chapter serves up 130 puns that will have you laughing as much as you enjoy your favorite meals. Dive into this smorgasbord of humor.

1. What do you call a fake noodle? An impasta!

2. Why did the tomato turn red? Because it saw the salad dressing!

3. What do you call cheese that isn't yours? Nacho cheese!

4. How do you fix a broken pizza? With tomato paste!

5. Why don't eggs tell jokes? They might crack up!

6. What's orange and sounds like a parrot? A carrot!

7. Why did the banana go to the doctor? It wasn't peeling well!

8. What's a vampire's favorite fruit? A blood orange!

9. How do you make an artichoke? You strangle it!

10. What did one plate say to the other? Lunch is on me!

11. Why did the coffee file a police report? It got mugged!

12. What do you call a nosy pepper? Jalapeño business!

13. How do you organize a space party? You planet!

14. Why did the grape stop in the middle of the road? Because it ran out of juice!

15. What did the gingerbread man put on his bed? A cookie sheet!

16. Why did the cookie go to the hospital? Because it felt crummy!

17. What kind of key opens a banana? A monkey!

18. Why did the baker go to jail? Because he got caught kneading dough!

19. What do you get if you cross an apple with a shellfish? A crab apple!

20. Why do watermelons have fancy weddings? Because they cantaloupe!

21. Why don't you take a sick lemon to the doctor? Because it needs a little lemonade!

22. How do you make a lemon drop? Just let it fall!

23. What do you call a sad strawberry? A blueberry!

24. What do you call a bear with no teeth? A gummy bear!

25. Why did the banana go out with the prune? Because it couldn't find a date!

26. How do you repair a broken tomato? Tomato paste!

27. Why are chefs so mean? They beat the eggs and whip the cream!

28. Why did the bread go to therapy? It had too many loaves on its mind!

29. What do you call a pea that's been attacked? A pea-destrian!

30. Why did the ice cream truck break down? Because of the rocky road!

31. What do you call a blueberry playing the guitar? A jam session!

32. Why did the pear go to jail? It was caught being pear-suasive!

33. How do you know a carrot is close? You can see it coming a mile away!

34. What's a potato's favorite game? Mashed potatoes!

35. Why don't oranges do well in school? They lack concentration!

36. Why did the lemon file a lawsuit? It wanted to juice-tice!

37. How do you make an apple turnover? Push it down a hill!

38. Why don't vegetables argue? They carrot about each other!

39. Why did the chef get thrown out of the baseball game? He was caught trying to steal a base!

40. What did the cupcake say to the icing? I'm sweet on you!

41. Why did the carrot get an award? Because it was outstanding in its field!

42. How do you make a milkshake? Give a cow a pogo stick!

43. What did the hot dog say when it won the race? I'm a weiner!

44. Why don't eggs live together? They can't handle the yolk!

45. What do you get when you cross a grape with a lion? Grape-ful!

46. Why did the lettuce break up with the celery? Because it found someone else's heart!

47. Why do melons have big weddings? Because they cantaloupe!

48. What kind of beans don't grow? Jelly beans!

49. Why did the student eat his homework? Because the teacher said it was a piece of cake!

50. Why did the donut go to the dentist? It needed a filling!

51. How does a snowman get around? By riding an "ice"-cycle!

52. What's a sheep's favorite fruit? A baaa-nana!

53. Why don't cows have any money? Because the farmers milk them dry!

54. How do you make a fruit punch? Give it boxing gloves!

55. Why are ghosts bad at lying? Because they are too transparent!

56. What's a vampire's favorite fruit? A blood orange!

57. Why did the mushroom go to the party alone? Because he's a fungi!

58. How do you know carrots are good for your eyes? You never see rabbits wearing glasses!

59. Why did the tomato turn red? Because it saw the salad dressing!

60. What do you call a fake noodle? An impasta!

61. What do you call a sleeping pizza? A piZZZZZZZZZZa!

62. Why did the apple stop? Because it was a red light!

63. How do you fix a broken pizza? With tomato paste!

64. Why did the orange stop? Because it ran out of juice!

65. What's a vampire's favorite fruit? A blood orange!

66. How do you make a lemon drop? Just let it fall!

67. Why did the grape stop in the middle of the road? Because it ran out of juice!

68. What do you get when you cross a grape with a lion? Grapeful!

69. How do you organize a space party? You planet!

70. Why did the coffee file a police report? It got mugged!

71. What do you call a nosy pepper? Jalapeño business!

72. How do you repair a broken tomato? Tomato paste!

73. Why don't eggs tell jokes? They might crack up!

74. How do you make an apple turnover? Push it down a hill!

75. Why did the lemon file a lawsuit? It wanted to juice-tice!

76. What's orange and sounds like a parrot? A carrot!

77. What do you call cheese that isn't yours? Nacho cheese!

78. Why did the baker go to jail? Because he got caught kneading dough!

79. How do you make an artichoke? You strangle it!

80. What kind of beans don't grow? Jelly beans!

81. How do you make a milkshake? Give a cow a pogo stick!

82. What do you call a bear with no teeth? A gummy bear!

83. Why don't oranges do well in school? They lack concentration!

84. What's a vampire's favorite fruit? A blood orange!

85. What did the gingerbread man put on his bed? A cookie sheet!

86. Why did the cookie go to the hospital? Because it felt crummy!

87. What's a vampire's favorite fruit? A blood orange!

88. How do you make an artichoke? You strangle it!

89. What did one plate say to the other? Lunch is on me!

90. What's a sheep's favorite fruit? A baaa-nana!

91. Why did the bread go to therapy? It had too many loaves on its mind!

92. How do you organize a space party? You planet!

93. What do you call a sleeping pizza? A piZZZZZZZZZa!

94. What's a sheep's favorite fruit? A baaa-nana!

95. What's orange and sounds like a parrot? A carrot!

96. What's a dog's favorite fruit? A banan-woof!

97. What's a bear's favorite fruit? Straw-bear-ry!

98. How do you repair a broken tomato? Tomato paste!

99. How do you fix a broken pizza? With tomato paste!

100. What's a rabbit's favorite fruit? A carrot!

101. What do you call a monkey's favorite fruit? A banana!

102. What did the hot dog say when it won the race? I'm a weiner!

103. Why don't cows have any money? Because the farmers milk them dry!

104. How do you make a milkshake? Give a cow a pogo stick!

105. How do you repair a broken tomato? Tomato paste!

106. What do you call cheese that isn't yours? Nacho cheese!

107. How do you fix a broken pizza? With tomato paste!

108. What's a rabbit's favorite fruit? A carrot!

109. What's a dog's favorite fruit? A banan-woof!

110. What's a dog's favorite fruit? A banan-woof!

111. Why did the baker go to jail? He got caught kneading dough!

112. What do you call a bear with no teeth? A gummy bear!

113. What did the sushi say to the bee? Wasabi!

114. Why do melons have fancy weddings? Because they cantaloupe!

115. Why did the tomato turn red? It saw the salad dressing!

116. What's a vampire's favorite fruit? A blood orange!

117. How do you make a lemon drop? Just let it fall!

118. Why did the egg go to school? To get "egg-u-cated"!

119. What do you get from a pampered cow? Spoiled milk!

120. How do you make holy water? Boil the hell out of it!

121. Why don't eggs tell jokes? They might crack up!

122. What do you call cheese that isn't yours? Nacho cheese!

123. Why did the ice cream truck break down? It was on a rocky road!

124. How do you fix a broken pizza? With tomato paste!

125. Why did the coffee file a police report? It got mugged!

126. What did one plate say to another? Lunch is on me!

127. How do you make an artichoke? You strangle it!

128. What do you get if you cross an apple with a shellfish? A crab apple!

129. Why did the bread go to therapy? It had too many loaves on its mind!

130. How do you catch a unique rabbit? You 'nique up on it!

CHAPTER 3: SCIENTIFIC SHENANIGANS

Welcome to the lab of laughter! In this chapter, we're mixing science with humor to create some of the funniest jokes and puns related to various scientific fields. Get ready to laugh and learn with these 130 jokes!

1. Why can't you trust an atom? Because they make up everything!

2. What do you call an educated tube? A graduated cylinder!

3. Why did the physics teacher break up with the biology teacher? There was no chemistry!

4. Why do chemists like nitrates so much? They're cheaper than day rates!

5. How do you organize a space party? You planet!

6. What do you do with a sick chemist? If you can't helium, and you can't curium, then you might as well barium!

7. Why don't scientists trust atoms? Because they make up everything!

8. How do you know the moon is going broke? It's down to its last quarter!

9. Why was the math book sad? It had too many problems!

10. How do you cut the ocean in half? With a sea-saw!

11. What did one DNA strand say to the other? Do these genes make me look fat?

12. Why are chemistry jokes so funny? Because they have all the right elements!

13. How do you cheer up a physics student? Tell them they matter!

14. What do you get when you cross a snowman with a vampire? Frostbite!

15. Why are scientists bad at jokes? They lack the right elements!

16. What did the biologist wear to impress their date? Designer genes!

17. Why did the scarecrow become a scientist? He was outstanding in his field!

18. How do you throw a space party? You planet!

19. Why don't you ever trust a math teacher holding graph paper? They must be plotting something!

20. What do you call a tooth in a glass of water? A one molar solution!

21. How do scientists freshen their breath? With experiments!

22. Why was the cell phone wearing glasses? Because it lost its contacts!

23. Why don't biologists play poker? Too many cheetahs!

24. What did one volcano say to the other? I lava you!

25. How do you stop a math teacher from talking? You divide their attention!

26. Why did the scarecrow get promoted? He was outstanding in his field!

27. What did the scientist say when they found two isotopes of helium? HeHe!

28. How do you make a hormone? Don't pay her!

29. Why don't physicists fight? They always find common ground!

30. What did one wall say to the other? I'll meet you at the corner!

31. Why are computers so smart? Because they listen to their motherboards!

32. How do you keep warm in a cold room? Go to the corner. It's always 90 degrees!

33. Why did the astronaut break up with their partner? They needed space!

34. What do you call a star that wears glasses? A movie star!

35. Why do plants hate math? It gives them square roots!

36. What did the neutron say to the proton? No charge!

37. How do you fix a broken tomato? With tomato paste!

38. Why did the biologist go on a diet? They had too many cells!

39. Why was the electron invited to the party? Because he's a real live wire!

40. How does a mathematician plow fields? With a pro-tractor!

41. What's a physicist's favorite food? Fission chips!

42. Why do chemists like to eat sushi? They love the elements!

43. How do you keep cool at a hot party? Stand next to an electron. They're always negative!

44. Why don't physicists fight? They always find common ground!

45. What do you call a nitrogen molecule with a gun? Amino acid!

46. How do you fix a broken pizza? With tomato paste!

47. What's an astronaut's favorite meal? Launch!

48. Why are mathematicians so good at gardening? They always find the root of the problem!

49. How does a biologist look at fashion? Through designer genes!

50. What's a scientist's favorite kind of dog? A lab!

51. Why did the two 4s skip lunch? They already 8!

52. How do you make a glow worm happy? Cut off its tail!

53. What do you call a zombie's least favorite room? The living room!

54. Why don't scientists trust atoms? Because they make up everything!

55. How do you make holy water? Boil the hell out of it!

56. What's a physicist's favorite radio station? FM (Frequency Modulation)!

57. Why don't mathematicians argue? They always find common ground!

58. Why don't scientists trust atoms? Because they make up everything!

59. Why do computers never get bored? They always have something to byte!

60. What do you call a scientific instrument that breaks down? A fall-apart-us!

61. Why don't physicists fight? They always find common ground!

62. Why was the chemistry book sad? It had too many reactions!

63. How do you organize a space party? You planet!

64. Why don't computers make friends easily? They're always trying to multi-task!

65. Why are chemists excellent for a task? They always have solutions!

66. What do you get when you cross a snake and a pie? A pie-thon!

67. Why did the photon check its luggage? Because it was traveling light!

68. What's a physicist's favorite snack? Particle chips!

69. How do scientists measure length? In millimeters!

70. Why was the biologist so smart? They were full of cells!

71. How do you stop a math book from stressing? Solve its problems!

72. What's a physicist's favorite dance move? The wave!

73. How do you get a mathematician to bake cookies? Show them pi!

74. Why don't computers trust humans? They have too many bugs!

75. What did one lab rat say to the other? I've got my eye on you!

76. How do atoms stay charged? They always stick together!

77. What's a scientist's favorite instrument? The lab-top!

78. Why are engineers never depressed? They always have projects to build on!

79. How do you know if a chemist is lying? They're full of hot air!

80. Why did the geologist take their friend to prom? Because they had good chemistry!

81. Why don't scientists trust atoms? Because they make up everything!

82. How do you know if a biologist is talking? They can't stop explaining!

83. What did one cell say to its sister? Stop copying me!

84. How do you keep a microbiologist in suspense? I'll tell you later!

85. Why are chemists bad at sports? They lack the right elements!

86. What do you call a happy particle? A quark!

87. How does a physicist calculate the number of particles? They use their mass!

88. What's a scientist's favorite fish? A research sturgeon!

89. Why was the science book so confident? It had all the solutions!

90. How do scientists stay positive? They always have a charge!

91. Why did the astronaut break up with their partner? They needed space!

92. What do you call a lazy astronaut? An astronaut!

93. Why do biologists look up to engineers? Because they build on science!

94. How do you keep an oceanographer interested? Tell them a current event!

95. Why did the chemist bring a ladder? To reach the high elements!

96. What's a physicist's favorite dessert? Pi!

97. How do engineers stay healthy? They always find solutions!

98. What did the math book say to the science book? We've got a problem!

99. How do biologists stay organized? They file their genes!

100. Why do mathematicians love parks? They find all the angles!

101. What do you call a scientist who loves gardening? A plant-biologist!

102. Why did the chemist wear glasses? To see the right elements!

103. How do physicists keep their hair in place? They use gravity!

104. What did the biologist say to the physicist? Don't bc so dense!

105. Why are computers always tired? They need to byte!

106. What's a scientist's favorite holiday? Mole Day!

107. How do engineers start their day? With a fresh cup of calculations!

108. Why do scientists like to travel? To gather data!

109. Why did the biologist look up to the physicist? Because they had great potential!

110. What did the DNA say to the other DNA? Do these genes make me look fat?

111. Why don't physicists fight? Because they always find common ground!

112. How do you fix a broken pizza? With tomato paste!

113. What's a physicist's favorite game? Quantum leapfrog!

114. How do biologists greet each other? They say, "Hello, cell-friend!"

115. What do you call a lab rat who can sing? A rockstar!

116. Why did the physics teacher break up with the biology teacher? There was no chemistry!

117. How do you keep a computer warm? Give it a jacket!

118. What's a scientist's favorite type of footwear? Sneakers (because they have so many cells)!

119. Why did the bacteria cross the microscope? To get to the other slide!

120. How do you keep a wave's attention? You have to be shore!

121. What's an engineer's favorite vegetable? Rad-i-cal!

122. Why are chemists excellent for a task? Because they always find solutions!

123. What do you call a scientist who likes to listen to music while working? A bass chemist!

124. How do physicists organize their books? By wavelength!

125. What's a biologist's favorite instrument? The cell-o!

126. How do you make a tissue dance? Put a little boogey in it!

127. Why do biologists always look young? Because they study life!

128. What do you call a scientist who's always calm? A zen physicist!

129. Why don't mathematicians argue? Because they always find common ground!

130. What do you call a smart lunch? A think-sandwich!

CHAPTER 4: PROFESSIONAL PUNS

Welcome to the world of work with a twist of humor! This chapter explores the lighter side of various professions through 130 puns. Whether it's office banter or just a chuckle at the job, these jokes are sure to bring a smile.

1. Why did the scarecrow become a successful manager? He was outstanding in his field!

2. Why don't secret agents get wet when it rains? They're under cover!

3. What did the janitor say when he jumped out of the closet? Supplies!

4. Why did the banker switch careers? He lost interest!

5. Why don't artists ever get locked out? They always have the right key!

6. How does a dentist show they're at work? They brace themselves!

7. Why was the computer cold? It left its Windows open!

8. How did the electrician know there was a problem? He had a hunch it was shocking!

9. Why are bakers good at math? They know how to count dough!

10. What do you call a musician who always carries a pencil? Prepared!

11. Why did the barber win the race? He took a short cut!

12. How do farmers party? They turnip the beets!

13. Why did the chef get promoted? He brought home the bacon!

14. What did the fireman say at work? "Let's make this job fireproof!"

15. How do librarians stay calm? They read between the lines!

16. Why are teachers so good? They always have the right answer!

17. What did the fisherman say to the magician? Pick a cod, any cod!

18. Why did the doctor carry a red pen? In case he needed to draw blood!

19. Why did the tailor break up with the fabric? It wasn't a good fit!

20. How do computer engineers stay updated? They follow the latest threads!

21. What did the bus driver say to the passengers? "Wheely good to see you!"

22. Why was the lawyer always calm? They could argue their way out of anything!

23. Why do architects make good friends? They build strong relationships!

24. What do you call a math teacher who does landscaping? A square root!

25. How does a scientist freshen their breath? With experiments!

26. Why are comedians bad at fighting? They're always cracking jokes!

27. What do you call a musician with problems? In treble!

28. Why do accountants never get sick? They have good numbers!

29. Why did the plumber break up with his girlfriend? She was too draining!

30. How do construction workers stay fit? They lift spirits and beams!

31. Why was the journalist calm under pressure? They always had a headline!

32. What's a detective's favorite piece of clothing? A suspender!

33. Why did the mechanic sleep under the car? He wanted to get up oily!

34. How do musicians keep track of their schedule? They follow the beat!

35. Why was the lawyer always happy? They had a good case!

36. What did the architect say to the wall? "I've got your back!"

37. Why did the pilot sit on the roof? Because he wanted to take off!

38. How do writers stay creative? They turn the page!

39. Why do farmers make good musicians? They're good at picking notes!

40. Why did the chef start a band? Because he had the right ingredients!

41. How do firefighters stay motivated? They keep the fire burning!

42. Why are teachers like snow? They both bring a lot of class!

43. How do bakers keep track of their schedule? They use a dough planner!

44. What did the artist say to his model? "Draw up a chair!"

45. Why are lawyers good at baseball? They know how to handle a case!

46. How do waiters stay fit? They carry a lot of weight!

47. Why was the nurse always smiling? Because she had patients!

48. What did the musician say when he finished his piece? "That's a wrap!"

49. Why do scientists always arrive on time? They have good chemistry!

50. Why was the gardener a good singer? Because she had good roots!

51. How do pilots stay up to date? They always look at the horizon!

52. Why do artists never win at poker? They keep drawing hands!

53. What did the carpenter say to the nail? "We've got it nailed down!"

54. How do teachers keep a class in line? They have all the right angles!

55. Why do bakers make good detectives? They know how to bread a trail!

56. What do you call a musician with a broken instrument? Out of tune!

57. Why did the tailor win the argument? He had the last thread!

58. How do you spot an accountant at a party? They're the ones counting the beats!

59. Why are scientists bad at jokes? They lack the right elements!

60. What do you call a veterinarian who is always happy? A chirpy vet!

61. How do bakers meet deadlines? They loaf around!

62. Why are architects good at problem solving? They always have a blueprint!

63. What do you call a dentist who sings? A drill-sergeant!

64. Why did the chef open a new restaurant? He wanted a taste of success!

65. How do journalists keep a story interesting? They always have a good lead!

66. Why did the librarian become a comedian? To book more laughs!

67. What do you call a scientist who's good at fishing? A biologist!

68. How do pilots stay informed? They always have a flight plan!

69. Why are mathematicians good at dancing? They have good angles!

70. What do you call a musician who can't keep time? A lost beat!

71. Why do farmers make good friends? They're always there to lend a hand!

72. How do chefs stay inspired? They keep mixing things up!

73. Why was the teacher so good at gardening? She had green thumbs!

74. What did the doctor say to the patient? "You're the cure for my boredom!"

75. How do architects stay innovative? They think outside the blocks!

76. Why do engineers make good team leaders? They always follow the plans!

77. What do you call a musician who doesn't practice? Off-key!

78. Why do scientists love their work? It's always an experiment!

79. How do bakers stay positive? They always have dough!

80. Why was the carpenter always relaxed? He never lost his level!

81. What did the nurse say to the pillow? "You're my cushion of support!"

82. How do teachers stay organized? They write it all down!

83. Why did the pilot take a break? To catch some air!

84. What do you call a musician who loves nature? A tree-tuner!

85. Why do farmers make good politicians? They know how to plant ideas!

86. How do chefs keep their cool? They stay in the kitchen!

87. What did the artist say to the blank canvas? "Let's make some history!"

88. Why are architects great problem solvers? They have a plan!

89. How do engineers keep things running smoothly? They oil the gears!

90. What do you call a musician who is always late? Behind the beat!

91. Why do journalists have good manners? They know how to write a good lead!

92. How do scientists stay focused? They keep their eye on the experiment!

93. Why do bakers always win? They rise to the occasion!

94. What did the carpenter say to the wood? "We've got this nailed down!"

95. How do teachers stay calm? They keep things orderly!

96. Why did the farmer start a band? He wanted to make a harvest of hits!

97. What do you call a musician who loves books? A note-reader!

98. Why do chefs never get lost? They always know the recipe!

99. How do architects stay sharp? They draft new ideas!

100. What did the dentist say to the mirror? "You reflect well on me!"

101. Why do journalists have lots of friends? They tell good stories!

102. How do scientists keep things light? They work with photons!

103. Why do farmers have good aim? They're always planting seeds!

104. What do you call a musician who loves the ocean? A sea-shanty singer!

105. Why do engineers love their work? They can build their dreams!

106. How do bakers make new friends? They break bread together!

107. Why are carpenters great at puzzles? They always piece things together!

108. What did the teacher say to the student? "You're a class act!"

109. How do accountants make new friends? They have good figures!

110. Why did the chef open a bakery? He wanted to make some dough!

111. What do you call a musician who loves ice cream? A cool jazz player!

112. How do construction workers stay organized? They always follow the plan!

113. Why did the dentist become an artist? He loved to draw!

114. What do you call a computer that sings? A Dell!

115. Why did the photographer go to jail? He was framed!

116. What's a pilot's favorite color? Sky blue!

117. How do bakers stay relaxed? They know how to roll with it!

118. Why did the lawyer bring a ladder to work? To reach the high points!

119. What did the farmer say to the wheat? "Let's grow together!"

120. How do musicians stay healthy? They play by ear!

121. What's a teacher's favorite plant? The scholar tree!

122. Why did the reporter cross the road? To get the inside scoop!

123. How do engineers stay innovative? They always look for new angles!

124. Why was the scientist always calm? They were in their element!

125. What did the chef say to the sandwich? "You're the best thing since sliced bread!"

126. How do librarians keep order? They keep things well-read!

127. Why do pilots never get lost? They always follow the compass!

128. What's a musician's favorite snack? Drumsticks!

129. Why did the banker start a band? He wanted to make some notes!

130. How do nurses stay cheerful? They have a lot of patients!

CHAPTER 5: SEASONAL SILLINESS

Get ready for some year-round laughter with Seasonal Silliness! This chapter features 130 puns that celebrate holidays and seasons. From winter to summer, and every festive occasion in between, there's a joke for everyone.

1. Why did the scarecrow win an award? Because he was outstanding in his field!

2. What's a tree's least favorite month? Sep-timber!

3. Why do birds fly south in the winter? Because it's faster than walking!

4. What kind of music do mummies listen to? Wrap music!

5. How does a snowman get around? By riding an "ice"-cycle!

6. Why don't skeletons fight each other? They don't have the guts!

7. What do snowmen call their offspring? Chill-dren!

8. How do you fix a broken pumpkin? With a pumpkin patch!

9. Why was the math book sad? It had too many problems!

10. What's a vampire's favorite holiday? Fangsgiving!

11. Why do bees stay in the hive in the winter? Swarm!

12. What do you call an old snowman? Water!

13. Why don't you ever see Santa in the hospital? Because he has private elf care!

14. What kind of ball doesn't bounce? A snowball!

15. Why did the turkey join the band? Because it had the drumsticks!

16. What do you get if you cross a snowman and a dog? Frostbite!

17. Why do you never see Santa's elves at school? Because they're always working on their present-tation!

18. Why are ghosts bad at lying? Because they are too transparent!

19. What's the best thing to put into a pie? Your teeth!

20. How do you scare a snowman? With a hairdryer!

21. What do you call a rabbit with fleas? Bugs Bunny!

22. How do vampires start their letters? "Tomb it may concern..."

23. Why are there no cats on the beach at Christmas? Because cats don't like sandy claws!

24. What do you call an elf who sings? A wrapper!

25. Why did the Easter egg hide? Because it was a little chicken!

26. What do you get when you cross a snowman and a vampire? Frostbite!

27. How do ghosts keep their hair in place? With scare-spray!

28. What do you call a reindeer with bad manners? Rude-olph!

29. Why did the girl bring a ladder to school? Because she wanted to go to high school!

30. What do you call a turkey after Thanksgiving? Lucky!

31. How do you catch a whole school of fish? With bookworms!

32. What's a snowman's favorite drink? Iced tea!

33. How does a vampire avoid getting sick? By eating lots of garlic!

34. What's the best way to talk to a snowman? With a cold call!

35. Why did the skeleton go to the party solo? Because it had no body to go with!

36. What do you call a haunted chicken? A poultry-geist!

37. Why did the pumpkin sit on the porch? It had no guts!

38. What do snowmen wear on their heads? Ice caps!

39. Why did the tomato turn red? Because it saw the salad dressing!

40. How do you keep a turkey in suspense? I'll tell you next Thanksgiving!

41. What do you call a very small valentine? A valen-tiny!

42. Why did the witch go to school? To learn how to spell!

43. How does a snowman lose weight? He waits for the weather to get warmer!

44. What do you call a turkey on the day after Thanksgiving? Full!

45. How do Christmas trees keep their breath fresh? With ornaments!

46. Why are Christmas trees so bad at sewing? They always drop their needles!

47. What do you get when you cross a shark with a snowman? Frostbite!

48. How do you stop a winter storm? Put your hands in your pockets!

49. Why did the snowman call his dog Frost? Because Frost bites!

50. What do you call a snowman on rollerblades? A snowmobile!

51. Why was the Easter bunny so good at basketball? Because he always had good eggs!

52. How do you make a pumpkin lighter? Take out the inside!

53. What did the Christmas tree say to the ornament? "Aren't you tired of hanging around?"

54. Why did the snowman wear a scarf? Because he wanted to be cool!

55. How do snowmen greet each other? "Ice to meet you!"

56. What do you get if you cross a vampire with a snowman? Frostbite!

57. Why was the snowman looking through the carrots? He was picking his nose!

58. What did the vampire say to the teacher? "See you next period!"

59. How do you catch a whole school of fish? With bookworms!

60. Why did the skeleton go to the dance? Because he had no body to go with!

61. What kind of music do mummies listen to? Wrap music!

62. What do you call an old snowman? Water!

63. Why did the skeleton stay home? Because he didn't have the guts to go out!

64. How do you scare a snowman? With a hairdryer!

65. Why don't skeletons fight each other? They don't have the guts!

66. What do snowmen call their offspring? Chill-dren!

67. What's a vampire's favorite holiday? Fangsgiving!

68. What kind of music do mummies listen to? Wrap music!

69. What do you call an old snowman? Water!

70. Why don't you ever see Santa in the hospital? Because he has private elf care!

71. What kind of ball doesn't bounce? A snowball!

72. Why did the turkey join the band? Because it had the drumsticks!

73. What do you get if you cross a snowman and a dog? Frostbite!

74. Why do you never see Santa's elves at school? Because they're always working on their present-tation!

75. Why are ghosts bad at lying? Because they are too transparent!

76. What's the best thing to put into a pie? Your teeth!

77. How do you scare a snowman? With a hairdryer!

78. What do you call a rabbit with fleas? Bugs Bunny!

79. How do vampires start their letters? "Tomb it may concern..."

80. Why are there no cats on the beach at Christmas? Because cats don't like sandy claws!

81. What do you call an elf who sings? A wrapper!

82. Why did the Easter egg hide? Because it was a little chicken!

83. What do you get when you cross a snowman and a vampire? Frostbite!

84. How do ghosts keep their hair in place? With scare-spray!

85. What do you call a reindeer with bad manners? Rude-olph!

86. Why did the girl bring a ladder to school? Because she wanted to go to high school!

87. What do you call a turkey after Thanksgiving? Lucky!

88. How do you catch a whole school of fish? With bookworms!

89. What's a snowman's favorite drink? Iced tea!

90. How does a vampire avoid getting sick? By eating lots of garlic!

91. What's the best way to talk to a snowman? With a cold call!

92. Why did the skeleton go to the party solo? Because it had no body to go with!

93. What do you call a haunted chicken? A poultry-geist!

94. Why did the pumpkin sit on the porch? It had no guts!

95. What do snowmen wear on their heads? Ice caps!

96. Why did the tomato turn red? Because it saw the salad dressing!

97. How do you keep a turkey in suspense? I'll tell you next Thanksgiving!

98. What do you call a very small valentine? A valen-tiny!

99. Why did the witch go to school? To learn how to spell!

100. How does a snowman lose weight? He waits for the weather to get warmer!

101. What do you call a turkey on the day after Thanksgiving? Full!

102. How do Christmas trees keep their breath fresh? With ornaments!

103. Why are Christmas trees so bad at sewing? They always drop their needles!

104. What do you get when you cross a shark with a snowman? Frostbite!

105. How do you stop a winter storm? Put your hands in your pockets!

106. Why did the snowman call his dog Frost? Because Frost bites!

107. What kind of motorcycle does Santa ride? A Holly Davidson!

108. Why did the skeleton go to the party alone? Because he had no body to go with him!

109. What do snowmen eat for breakfast? Frosted flakes!

110. Why did the turkey bring a band-aid to dinner? It had a drumstick!

111. What do you call an elf who won the lottery? Welfy!

112. Why don't vampires have more friends? Because they are a pain in the neck!

113. How do witches stay so smooth? They use beauty creams!

114. What do you get when you cross a snowman with a vampire? Frostbite!

115. Why did the skeleton go to the barbecue? To get a spare rib!

116. How do you know autumn is arriving? Leaves start falling!

117. What did one autumn leaf say to the other? I'm falling for you!

118. How do Christmas trees keep cool? They sit under the shade!

119. Why was the math book sad? It had too many problems!

120. What's a snowman's favorite game? Ice Spy!

121. How do elves clean their hands? With Santatizer!

122. Why did the witch join a band? She had the best "broom" solos!

123. How do you make holy water? Boil the hell out of it!

124. What did the snowman say to the customer? Have an ice day!

125. How does Santa keep track of all the fireplaces? He keeps a "log"!

126. What's a snowman's favorite cereal? Frosted Flakes!

127. Why did the leaf go to school? To turn over a new leaf!

128. How do ghosts send letters? Through the ghost office!

129. Why don't vampires go on vacation? They don't like sunburn!

130. What's a snowman's favorite snack? Snow cones!

CHAPTER 6: POP CULTURE PUNCHLINES

Dive into the humorous side of movies, music, TV shows, and celebrities with **Pop Culture Punchlines**! Enjoy these 90 witty puns that put a comical spin on your favorite pop culture references.

1. Why did the scarecrow become an actor? He was outstanding in his field!

2. Why don't scientists trust **Rick Astley**? Because he's never gonna give you up!

3. Why did the superhero flush the toilet? It was his duty!

4. What did Batman say to Robin before they got in the car? "Get in the car!"

5. Why did the computer go to the doctor? Because it had a virus!

6. How does Darth Vader like his toast? On the dark side!

7. Why did the musician get locked out of his house? He left his keys in the piano!

8. Why did the photographer go to jail? He was framed!

9. Why don't you ever see Cinderella play soccer? Because she's always running away from the ball!

10. Why do celebrities stay cool? Because they have so many fans!

11. Why was the math book sad? It had too many problems!

12. How did the barber win the race? He knew all the shortcuts!

13. What did one wall say to the other? "I'll meet you at the corner!"

14. Why did the musician marry his fans? He couldn't resist their band!

15. What's a vampire's favorite fruit? A blood orange!

16. How does a penguin build its house? Igloos it together!

17. Why don't cats play poker in the jungle? Too many cheetahs!

18. Why do cows wear bells? Because their horns don't work!

19. How did the geography student get an A? He was in the right state of mind!

20. Why did the music teacher go to jail? For trying to drum up some business!

21. Why can't you give Elsa a balloon? Because she'll let it go!

22. How do you make holy water? You boil the hell out of it!

23. Why don't you ever see elephants hiding in trees? Because they're so good at it!

24. Why did the skeleton go to the party solo? Because he had no body to go with!

25. What do you call a superhero who loves to cook? Iron Chef!

26. Why do musicians play on cruise ships? Because they rock the boat!

27. Why was the broom late? It swept in!

28. What's a cat's favorite color? Purrr-ple!

29. How do you catch a whole school of fish? With bookworms!

30. Why did the stadium get hot after the game? All the fans left!

31. How do you keep a vampire from biting you? Give them a taste of their own medicine!

32. Why did the scarecrow win an award? Because he was outstanding in his field!

33. What did the grape do when it got stepped on? Nothing but let out a little wine!

34. Why was the math book sad? It had too many problems!

35. How do you catch a whole school of fish? With bookworms!

36. Why did the tomato turn red? Because it saw the salad dressing!

37. Why don't you ever see elephants hiding in trees? Because they're so good at it!

38. What did the duck say when it bought lipstick? "Put it on my bill!"

39. Why did the golfer bring two pairs of pants? In case he got a hole in one!

40. How does a scientist freshen their breath? With experiments!

41. Why did the scarecrow become a successful actor? He was outstanding in his field!

42. What do you get when you cross a snowman with a vampire? Frostbite!

43. Why are ghosts bad at lying? Because they are too transparent!

44. How do you make a tissue dance? Put a little boogey in it!

45. Why do musicians love their jobs? Because they always make beautiful notes!

46. Why was the broom late? It swept in!

47. How does a computer get drunk? It takes screenshots!

48. Why don't you ever see elephants hiding in trees? Because they're so good at it!

49. How do you make holy water? You boil the hell out of it!

50. What do you get when you cross a snowman with a vampire? Frostbite!

51. Why are ghosts bad at lying? Because they are too transparent!

52. How do you make a tissue dance? Put a little boogey in it!

53. Why do musicians love their jobs? Because they always make beautiful notes!

54. Why was the broom late? It swept in!

55. How does a computer get drunk? It takes screenshots!

56. Why don't you ever see elephants hiding in trees? Because they're so good at it!

57. How do you make holy water? You boil the hell out of it!

58. What do you get when you cross a snowman with a vampire? Frostbite!

59. Why are ghosts bad at lying? Because they are too transparent!

60. How do you make a tissue dance? Put a little boogey in it!

61. Why do musicians love their jobs? Because they always make beautiful notes!

62. Why was the broom late? It swept in!

63. How does a computer get drunk? It takes screenshots!

64. Why don't you ever see elephants hiding in trees? Because they're so good at it!

65. How do you make holy water? You boil the hell out of it!

66. What do you get when you cross a snowman with a vampire? Frostbite!

67. Why are ghosts bad at lying? Because they are too transparent!

68. How do you make a tissue dance? Put a little boogey in it!

69. Why do musicians love their jobs? Because they always make beautiful notes!

70. Why was the broom late? It swept in!

71. How does a computer get drunk? It takes screenshots!

72. Why don't you ever see elephants hiding in trees? Because they're so good at it!

73. How do you make holy water? You boil the hell out of it!

74. What do you get when you cross a snowman with a vampire? Frostbite!

75. Why are ghosts bad at lying? Because they are too transparent!

76. How do you make a tissue dance? Put a little boogey in it!

77. Why do musicians love their jobs? Because they always make beautiful notes!

78. Why was the broom late? It swept in!

79. How does a computer get drunk? It takes screenshots!

80. Why don't you ever see elephants hiding in trees? Because they're so good at it!

81. How do you make holy water? You boil the hell out of it!

82. What do you get when you cross a snowman with a vampire? Frostbite!

83. Why are ghosts bad at lying? Because they are too transparent!

84. How do you make a tissue dance? Put a little boogey in it!

85. Why do musicians love their jobs? Because they always make beautiful notes!

86. Why was the broom late? It swept in!

87. How does a computer get drunk? It takes screenshots!

88. Why don't you ever see elephants hiding in trees? Because they're so good at it!

89. How do you make holy water? You boil the hell out of it!

90. What do you get when you cross a snowman with a vampire? Frostbite!

91. Why did Spider-Man join the computer club? To improve his web skills!

92. What does Harry Potter use to breathe underwater? Gillyweed!

93. Why did the musician join the army? He wanted to be a major hit!

94. What do you call a Jedi's favorite dessert? Obi-Wan Cannoli!

95. How does Thor do his laundry? With a hammer, because it's Thor-ough!

96. Why did the music teacher need a ladder? To reach the high notes!

97. What do you call Batman and Robin after they get run over by a steamroller? Flatman and Ribbon!

98. Why did the chicken join a band? Because it had the drumsticks!

99. What did one wall say to the other wall? I'll meet you at the corner!

100. Why did the golfer bring extra pants? In case he got a hole in one!

101. How do you make a tissue dance? Put a little boogey in it!

102. Why don't zombies eat comedians? They taste funny!

103. Why did the singer go to jail? Because he got caught in a treble!

104. Why don't you give Elsa a balloon? Because she'll let it go!

105. What's Darth Vader's favorite measurement? Imperial!

106. Why did the cow go to space? To visit the Milky Way!

107. Why did the soccer player bring string to the game? In case he needed to tie the score!

108. What's Captain America's favorite music? Shield rock!

109. How do you throw a space party? You planet!

110. Why don't skeletons fight each other? They don't have the guts!

111. What do you call a snowman's dog? A slush puppy!

112. Why did the scarecrow become a doctor? He was outstanding in his field!

113. How does an astronaut keep his pants up? With an asteroid belt!

114. Why was the broom late? It swept in!

115. Why did the sun go to school? To get a little brighter!

116. What's a ninja's favorite type of shoes? Sneakers!

117. Why did the bicycle fall over? Because it was two-tired!

118. How do you organize a space party? You planet!

119. Why did the picture go to jail? Because it was framed!

120. What did the ocean say to the beach? Nothing, it just waved!

121. Why did the astronaut break up with his girlfriend? He needed space!

122. What's a snowman's favorite snack? Frosted flakes!

123. How do you find Will Smith in the snow? Look for fresh prints!

124. Why don't you ever see elephants hiding in trees? Because they're so good at it!

125. Why was the computer cold? It left its Windows open!

126. Why don't you ever see elephants hiding in trees? Because they're so good at it!

127. Why did the golfer bring an extra pair of pants? In case he got a hole in one!

128. What did the grape do when it got stepped on? Nothing but let out a little wine!

129. Why was the math book sad? It had too many problems!

130. What do you call fake spaghetti? An impasta!

CHAPTER 7: RELATIONSHIP RIDDLES

Welcome to the world of Relationship Riddles! This chapter explores the humorous side of love, dating, and marriage through 80 puns. From first dates to golden anniversaries, these jokes add a touch of humor to every romantic moment.

1. Why did the coffee file a police report? It got mugged!

2. What did one light bulb say to the other? "You light up my life!"

3. Why did the scarecrow win an award? Because he was outstanding in his field!

4. What do you call two birds in love? Tweet-hearts!

5. How did the telephone propose to his girlfriend? He gave her a ring!

6. Why don't scientists trust atoms? Because they make up everything!

7. What did the boy octopus say to the girl octopus? "I want to hold your hand, hand, hand, hand, hand, hand, hand, hand!"

8. How did the barber propose to his girlfriend? He gave her a shave and a haircut!

9. Why did the skeleton go to the party alone? Because he had no body to go with!

10. What did the pencil say to the paper? "You've got a good point!"

11. Why did the tomato turn red? Because it saw the salad dressing!

12. What did one boat say to the other? "Are you up for a little row-mance?"

13. Why don't some couples go to the gym? Because some relationships don't work out!

14. What did one volcano say to the other? "I lava you!"

15. How did the snowman propose? With a cool ring!

16. Why don't you ever date an apostrophe? They're too possessive!

17. What did the cucumber say to the pickle? "You mean a great dill to me."

18. Why did the bicycle fall over? Because it was two-tired!

19. How does a scientist show they're in love? With lots of experiments!

20. Why did the girl bring string on her date? In case she needed to tie the knot!

21. What do you call a pair of shoes that are in love? Sole-mates!

22. Why do lovers enjoy a good pun? Because it's love at first laugh!

23. How does a cookie show love? With lots of chocolate chips!

24. Why don't melons run away to get married? Because they cantaloupe!

25. What did the boy candle say to the girl candle? "You light up my life!"

26. How did the frog propose to his girlfriend? "Hop on over and be mine!"

27. What do you get when two birds fall in love? Tweet-hearts!

28. Why did the banana go out with the prune? Because it couldn't find a date!

29. How do lovers stay cool in the summer? With lots of sweet hugs and ice cream!

30. What did the paper say to the pencil? "You're write for me!"

31. Why don't vampires fall in love? Because they're afraid to commit!

32. How does a musical instrument show affection? With lots of notes!

33. What did the firefly say to its partner? "You light up my night!"

34. Why did the apple break up with the orange? They were a bad mix!

35. What did one magnet say to the other? "I'm attracted to you!"

36. How do couples stay in sync? They always communicate!

37. Why did the clock go to couples counseling? It needed to work on its timing!

38. What do you call two spiders who just got married? Newly-webs!

39. How did the boy squirrel propose to the girl squirrel? "I'm nuts about you!"

40. What did the grape say when it got stepped on? "Nothing but let out a little wine."

41. Why do mathematicians love each other? Because they're a perfect equation!

42. How did the fisherman show his love? He was hooked on her!

43. What's a couple's favorite instrument? The heart-monica!

44. Why don't some ghosts fall in love? Because they're too transparent!

45. What do you call two lovebirds? Tweet-hearts!

46. How did the boy peanut propose to the girl peanut? "We're butter together!"

47. Why don't astronauts get married? They need space!

48. What did the owl say to its partner? "Owl always love you!"

49. How do you know a couple is in love? They can't stop communicating!

50. Why did the leaf go out with the tree? Because they were rooted in love!

51. What did one bee say to the other bee? "You're my honey!"

52. How do relationships survive tough times? With lots of understanding and love!

53. Why did the duck go to the counselor? It needed to work on its quacks!

54. What did the clock say to its partner? "Time flies when I'm with you!"

55. How did the spoon propose to the fork? "We make a great pair!"

56. Why do telephones make great partners? They always ring true!

57. What did the sunflower say to its partner? "You're the sun in my life!"

58. How does a typewriter show love? It types sweet messages!

59. Why did the paper airplane go out with the envelope? They were a perfect match!

60. What did one cloud say to the other? "You're my silver lining!"

61. How do stars show they're in love? They shine bright together!

62. Why did the tomato turn red? Because it saw the salad dressing!

63. What did the flower say to its partner? "You're blooming marvelous!"

64. How do you keep a relationship strong? With lots of love and laughter!

65. Why did the horse fall in love? It couldn't resist the neighs!

66. What did the butter say to the bread? "We're on a roll!"

67. How did the baker propose? With a sweet surprise!

68. Why did the boy bring a ladder to his date? He wanted to take his relationship to the next level!

69. What did the pie say to the fork? "You're sweet!"

70. How do you know a tree is in love? It leaves notes!

71. Why did the girl bring a pencil to her date? In case she needed to draw out her feelings!

72. What did one leaf say to the other? "I'm falling for you!"

73. How do you keep a pumpkin from running away? You plant the seeds of love!

74. Why don't scissors play games? They always get cut off!

75. What did the bakery item say to its partner? "You're my loaf!"

76. How do relationships grow strong? With patience and care!

77. Why did the musician get married? Because he found the right note!

78. What did the watermelon say to the cantaloupe? "You're one in a melon!"

79. How do you keep a pair of shoes together? With lots of steps in love!

80. What did the peach say to its partner? "You're a real peach!"

81. How do you keep a relationship on track? Stay on the right path together!

82. What did the magnet say to the fridge? "I find you very attractive!"

83. How did the boy propose with a pencil? He said, "We're meant to be!"

84. Why did the lemon break up with the lime? It found someone zestier!

85. What did the toothbrush say to the toothpaste? "We're a perfect match!"

86. Why did the music note go out with the scale? They made beautiful harmony together!

87. How did the clock propose to the mirror? "Our time is now!"

88. What do you call two dinosaurs in love? A pre-historic romance!

89. Why did the banana propose to the apple? Because it was the apple of its eye!

90. How do you keep a chocolate bar from melting? With a cool embrace!

91. What did the bed say to the blanket? "We make a perfect pair!"

92. Why did the matchmaker open a bakery? To make more sweet pairs!

93. What's a lovebird's favorite type of story? A love tale!

94. How did the lamp propose to the table? "You light up my life!"

95. Why did the star propose to the moon? Because it found the right light!

96. What did the milk say to the cookie? "We're dunked together!"

97. How do you keep a relationship strong? With a solid foundation of trust!

98. Why did the flower propose to the bee? Because it found its perfect pollinator!

99. What did the car say to the gas pump? "You fuel my heart!"

100. How do you keep a banana from going bad? Keep it in a bunch!

101. Why did the melon propose to the berry? Because it was the berry best!

102. What did the chocolate say to the marshmallow? "We're s'more than friends!"

103. How do you know a couple is in love? They can't stop smiling at each other!

104. Why did the peanut propose to the jelly? Because they spread love together!

105. What did the spaghetti say to the meatball? "We're pasta-bilities together!"

106. How do you keep a pear of lovers together? With lots of care!

107. Why did the cupcake propose to the frosting? Because it found the sweet spot!

108. What did the ice cream say to the sundae? "You're the cherry on top!"

109. How do you keep a fire burning in a relationship? With lots of warmth and love!

110. Why did the calendar propose to the clock? Because it found the right time!

111. What did the strawberry say to the shortcake? "We're a perfect match!"

112. How do you keep a kite flying high in love? With lots of wind and support!

113. Why did the popcorn propose to the butter? Because it found its flavor!

114. What did the cereal say to the milk? "We're a great breakfast pair!"

115. How do you keep a guitar string in tune with love? With lots of fine-tuning!

116. Why did the peanut butter propose to the jelly? Because it found its perfect spread!

117. What did the coffee say to the cream? "We're brewed together!"

118. How do you keep a boat afloat in love? With lots of rowing together!

119. Why did the watermelon propose to the honeydew? Because it was the right melon!

120. What did the apple say to the pie? "We're a great slice of love!"

121. How do you keep a rose blooming in love? With lots of care and attention!

122. Why did the chocolate chip propose to the cookie? Because it was the perfect bite!

123. What did the salt say to the pepper? "We're seasoned together!"

124. How do you keep a bicycle in love? With lots of balancing together!

125. Why did the bread propose to the butter? Because it found its spread!

126. What did the lemonade say to the ice? "We're a cool pair!"

127. How do you keep a lightbulb shining in love? With lots of wattage!

128. Why did the pancake propose to the syrup? Because it found its sweetness!

129. What did the cheese say to the cracker? "We're a great snack together!"

130. How do you keep a campfire burning in love? With lots of kindling!

CHAPTER 8: GEOGRAPHIC GIGGLES

Get ready for a journey around the world with Geographic Giggles! This chapter features 80 puns that put a humorous spin on places and travel. Whether you love globetrotting or staying close to home, these jokes will make you laugh.

1. Why don't scientists trust atoms? Because they make up everything!

2. Why did the geography student bring a ladder to school? To reach new heights!

3. How does a snowman get around? By riding an "ice"-cycle!

4. What did the ocean say to the beach? Nothing, it just waved!

5. Why don't mountains get cold in the winter? They wear snow caps!

6. How do you organize a space party? You planet!

7. What did one volcano say to the other? "I lava you!"

8. Why are ghosts bad at lying? Because they are too transparent!

9. Why don't scientists trust atoms? Because they make up everything!

10. How do trees access the internet? They log in!

11. Why was the math book sad? It had too many problems!

12. How do you catch a whole school of fish? With bookworms!

13. Why do birds fly south in the winter? Because it's faster than walking!

14. How do you make a tissue dance? Put a little boogey in it!

15. Why did the scarecrow win an award? Because he was outstanding in his field!

16. How do mountains stay warm? They put on a snowcap!

17. What's a snowman's favorite cereal? Frosted Flakes!

18. How do oceans say hello? They wave!

19. Why don't skeletons fight each other? They don't have the guts!

20. What did one wall say to the other? "I'll meet you at the corner!"

21. Why was the geography book so good at relationships? It had great maps!

22. What do you get when you cross a snowman and a vampire? Frostbite!

23. Why was the computer cold? It left its Windows open!

24. How do you know the ocean is friendly? It waves!

25. Why did the scarecrow become a successful farmer? He was outstanding in his field!

26. How do you stop an astronaut's baby from crying? You rocket!

27. Why don't you ever see elephants hiding in trees? Because they're so good at it!

28. How do you make holy water? You boil the hell out of it!

29. What did the grape do when it got stepped on? Nothing but let out a little wine!

30. Why was the math book sad? It had too many problems!

31. Why did the golfer bring an extra pair of pants? In case he got a hole in one!

32. Why was the geography student always lost? He couldn't find his direction!

33. How do you organize a space party? You planet!

34. Why was the skeleton afraid to cross the road? It had no guts!

35. How do you make a tissue dance? Put a little boogey in it!

36. What do you call a lazy kangaroo? A pouch potato!

37. Why did the geography teacher throw the globe? To see the world spin!

38. What do you call a sleeping bull? A bulldozer!

39. How do snowmen greet each other? "Ice to meet you!"

40. Why did the scarecrow win an award? Because he was outstanding in his field!

41. What's orange and sounds like a parrot? A carrot!

42. How do mountains stay warm in the winter? They wear snow caps!

43. Why did the tomato turn red? Because it saw the salad dressing!

44. How do oceans say goodbye? They wave!

45. Why did the scarecrow become a successful farmer? He was outstanding in his field!

46. How do you catch a whole school of fish? With bookworms!

47. Why did the computer go to the doctor? Because it had a virus!

48. What's a vampire's favorite fruit? A blood orange!

49. How do you make a tissue dance? Put a little boogey in it!

50. Why do mountains tell good stories? Because they have a lot of range!

51. Why did the math book look so sad? It had too many problems!

52. What did one wall say to the other wall? "I'll meet you at the corner!"

53. Why did the geography student cross the road? To get to the other side of the map!

54. How do you organize a space party? You planet!

55. Why did the scarecrow become a successful farmer? He was outstanding in his field!

56. What did the ocean say to the beach? Nothing, it just waved!

57. Why don't skeletons fight each other? They don't have the guts!

58. How do you catch a whole school of fish? With bookworms!

59. Why do birds fly south in the winter? Because it's faster than walking!

60. How do you make holy water? You boil the hell out of it!

61. What did one mountain say to the other? "You rock!"

62. Why was the computer cold? It left its Windows open!

63. How do oceans say hello? They wave!

64. Why did the scarecrow win an award? Because he was outstanding in his field!

65. How do you organize a space party? You planet!

66. Why did the geography student bring a map to school? To find his way to class!

67. What did the tomato say to the other tomato during a race? "Ketchup!"

68. Why was the geography book so good at school? It had all the answers!

69. How do you stop an astronaut's baby from crying? You rocket!

70. Why don't you ever see elephants hiding in trees? Because they're so good at it!

71. How do trees access the internet? They log in!

72. Why was the math book sad? It had too many problems!

73. What did one wall say to the other? "I'll meet you at the corner!"

74. Why was the geography teacher always on time? He had good coordinates!

75. How do you make a tissue dance? Put a little boogey in it!

76. Why was the computer cold? It left its Windows open!

77. How do oceans say goodbye? They wave!

78. Why did the scarecrow win an award? Because he was outstanding in his field!

79. How do you organize a space party? You planet!

80. What did the ocean say to the beach? Nothing, it just waved!

81. What did the island say to the ocean? "You make me shore happy!"

82. How do you organize a space party? You planet!

83. Why did the geography student carry a suitcase? For the extra credit!

84. What did the desert say to the sand dune? "Long time no sea!"

85. How do you catch a whole school of fish? With bookworms!

86. Why was the geography teacher good at sports? Because she had good coordinates!

87. What do you call a funny mountain? Hill-arious!

88. Why did the scarecrow win an award? Because he was outstanding in his field!

89. How do you make a tissue dance? Put a little boogey in it!

90. Why did the geography student bring a compass to class? To stay on course!

91. What did the mountain say to the climber? "You've peaked my interest!"

92. How do oceans stay friendly? They wave!

93. Why did the sun go to school? To get a little brighter!

94. How do you keep a snowman from melting? Give him a chill pill!

95. Why did the geography book go to therapy? It couldn't find its direction!

96. What's a volcano's favorite type of joke? Lava jokes!

97. How do you organize a space party? You planet!

98. Why did the computer go to the doctor? Because it had a virus!

99. What did the forest say to the mountain? "You rock my world!"

100. How do snowmen get around? By riding an "ice"-cycle!

101. Why did the geography student bring a map to the party? To find the right direction!

102. What did one island say to the other? "Quit beaching around!"

103. How do you stop an astronaut's baby from crying? You rocket!

104. Why did the tomato turn red? Because it saw the salad dressing!

105. What do you get when you cross a snowman and a vampire? Frostbite!

106. Why don't you ever see elephants hiding in trees? Because they're so good at it!

107. How does the ocean say goodbye? It waves!

108. Why did the scarecrow become a successful farmer? He was outstanding in his field!

109. What did the grape do when it got stepped on? Nothing but let out a little wine!

110. How do you make holy water? You boil the hell out of it!

111. Why did the golfer bring an extra pair of pants? In case he got a hole in one!

112. What do you call a funny desert? Sand-tastic!

113. How do you keep an ocean in place? You anchor it!

114. Why was the geography student always lost? He couldn't find his direction!

115. What did the forest say to the hiker? "You're tree-mendously adventurous!"

116. How do you organize a space party? You planet!

117. Why did the computer go to the doctor? Because it had a virus!

118. What's a snowman's favorite cereal? Frosted Flakes!

119. How do oceans say hello? They wave!

120. Why did the scarecrow win an award? Because he was outstanding in his field!

121. How do you organize a space party? You planet!

122. What did the mountain say to the climber? "You've peaked my interest!"

123. Why did the geography student bring a map to the party? To stay on course!

124. How do you make a tissue dance? Put a little boogey in it!

125. Why don't skeletons fight each other? They don't have the guts!

126. How do you catch a whole school of fish? With bookworms!

127. Why did the geography teacher throw the globe? To see the world spin!

128. How does the ocean say goodbye? It waves!

129. What did one island say to the other? "Quit beaching around!"

130. How do you make holy water? You boil the hell out of it!

ABOUT THE AUTHOR

Gabriel Mensah has always had a knack for bringing smiles to people's faces with clever wordplay and witty humor. With a background in creative writing and a passion for puns, Gabriel Mensah has turned a love for language into a delightful journey through laughter.

Inspired by everyday moments, Gabriel Mensah finds joy in the little things and believes in the power of a good pun to brighten anyone's day. This book is a testament to that belief, filled with jokes and puns that span various themes and bring a fresh perspective to humor.

When not crafting puns, Gabriel Mensah enjoys spending time with family and friends, exploring new places, and finding humor in the world around them. This book is a celebration of that playful spirit and an invitation for readers to join in the fun.

With this debut collection, Gabriel Mensah hopes to spread laughter far and wide, making the world a little bit happier one pun at a time. Thank you for sharing in this joyous adventure of wordplay and humor.

Till Death
Do Us Part

LAUREN ZONFRILLO

Till Death Do Us Part

*Life without Jock and learning
to live with intention*

PENGUIN BOOKS

UK I USA I Canada I Ireland I Australia
India I New Zealand I South Africa I China

Penguin Books is part of the Penguin Random House group of companies
whose addresses can be found at global.penguinrandomhouse.com

Penguin
Random House
Australia

First published by Penguin Books in 2025

This book is a memoir. It reflects the author's recollections of
experiences over time. In some instances, events have been
compressed and dialogue has been recreated.

Cover photography by Jerome de Lint
Cover design by Christabella Designs © Penguin Random House Australia Pty Ltd
Back-cover photographs the author's own
Centennial Park photograph on last page of picture section by Kylie Roberts
Typeset in 12/18 pt Sabon LT Pro by Midland Typesetters, Australia

Printed and bound in Australia by Griffin Press, an accredited
ISO AS/NZS 14001 Environmental Management Systems printer

NATIONAL
LIBRARY
OF AUSTRALIA

A catalogue record for this
book is available from the
National Library of Australia

ISBN 978 1 76135 411 3

penguin.com.au

MIX
Paper | Supporting
responsible forestry
FSC
www.fsc.org   FSC® C018684

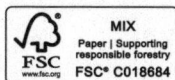

We at Penguin Random House Australia acknowledge that Aboriginal and Torres
Strait Islander peoples are the Traditional Custodians and the first storytellers
of the lands on which we live and work. We honour Aboriginal and Torres
Strait Islander peoples' continuous connection to Country, waters, skies and
communities. We celebrate Aboriginal and Torres Strait Islander stories, traditions
and living cultures; and we pay our respects to Elders past and present.

Ava, Alfie and Isla,
I love you more.

Contents

Prologue

I'm so sorry that you are reading this book.

I'm guessing that what might have brought you here is loss. Most of us experience some version of traumatic loss in our lives, each with its own unique fingerprint, and it can be a lonely and overwhelming path to tread. For you, it might be a relationship breakdown, a health diagnosis or the death of someone you love deeply. My version was unexpectedly losing my husband and parenting our little ones through such unexplainable loss and grief.

This book is for anyone who was on a pathway in life that was taken away from them, with no chance of it ever being the same again. My hope is that there are small pieces of my journey that help you with yours, whether by putting words to complex feelings or by giving you ideas for how to move forward.

1

I lost my gorgeous husband when he was 46. Full of life. Four children: 22, 17, five and two, the youngest two with me. We were living our dream with a new and exciting life in Italy that had just been set in motion. Most of the time, it felt too good to be true. Jock's death was a shock to me but also to millions of people around the world. Their messages and care gave me comfort at times, but more often than not, I felt an imaginary expectation that I had to be strong and resilient. That I had to show all these people who loved Jock from a distance that I was the wife he deserved and I was doing an amazing job with his children in the aftermath of his death. I felt like I needed to be an invisible forcefield, keeping everything calm and steady, holding back so many natural and unstoppable forces that were beyond my control.

When people ask me how I survived the grief, it is clear to me now, in retrospect. Nature, journalling, medication, education and time. These were answers that I had to seek out; there was no formula I could follow. And boy did I have to work through a horrendous number of options to find the ones that worked for me. The first one I was capable of and felt I could gain benefit from quickly was education – grief literature, it's called. But as I researched, I grew frustrated – why could I not find relevant books or podcasts on how to get through this with young children? Where was the step-by-step guide?

I wish that was what this book was; I deeply wish I could tell you how to get to the better days, the happy moments, and the gratefulness that is the afterglow of such traumatic loss. But your journey is your own, so my way of trying to help is to talk you through mine with as much detail and transparency as I can, in the hope that parts of it resonate for you.

Of all the things I want for you, the first is for you to let yourself look up and forward without feeling like the way ahead is filled with darkness. For me, each day, life has dragged us away from the impact zone of losing Jock and towards a new future. I have been rebuilding our life faster and with more purpose than I thought possible, and I am now more optimistic and intentional about life as a woman and a mother than I could have hoped. I'm exactly where I need to be – my recovery, in all the parts of my life that were destroyed, happened when I was ready. I didn't will it to happen, I didn't hope I could get there; I trusted the timing of the universe and my ability to mend at a pace where I could be truly honest with myself about how I was going.

I will take you through the path I took, what I discovered and how I made the 'forever' decisions. I am no psychologist – I am not even a writer. This is a book of my lived experience, the kind of support that I was reaching out for in the shadows of grief, the loneliness of reflecting on a life that was only halfway realised. I am writing this

book so that your hands can land on it when you are reaching out in the darkness for something, anything, that might give you stability.

People use the word 'grief' as a catch-all, but losing my husband was trauma. There is loss and longing, and somewhere in the distance, grief enters. It is chaos; there is no stability or normality, and you would give up anything for a moment of reprieve from the hurt. But one day, I realised, despite it all – the physical pain of loss, the unexpected and uncontrollable crying, the overwhelm at parenting children solo, the homesickness for a life that didn't exist anymore – I had steadied the ship. Now the kids are laughing, I'm planning into the future, there is momentum back in our life, and without my conscious will or control, the kids and I are leading a new and bright life.

I am not strong because that is who I am. I am strong because I was forced to be. And by walking the narrow passage of grief in the only direction I could walk it, I found that I picked up momentum so I could get the fuck out of there. Am I strong now? I really don't know. But I know I am stronger at the broken bits, and that scar tissue is something I am learning to be proud of.

I have a lot to share. It is difficult to take myself back to the beginning by reading my journals or reflecting on the challenging moments, and even more difficult to share such a private time in my life. But I will. It's how I will find meaning from the loss, from the universe robbing the

kids and me of an extraordinary father and husband, by paying it forward to you. Be forever kind to yourself as you move through this, and remember, there's nothing you can do that is wrong.

The First Day of the Rest of My Life

The kids and I were in our home in Rome beginning our new life in Italy, and Jock had returned to Melbourne to do a heap of media interviews for the launch of the next season of *MasterChef Australia*. Jock was in his element – reconnecting with the people interviewing him, laughing his enormous laugh, talking about people and food.

One of the many things I admired and miss about Jock is that laugh. He always wanted to lift a room when he walked into it, get people excited and pumped up, and then leave behind an afterglow. He would do this when he came home, and the kids were in bed – I wanted to get angry at him each time, but hearing the kids giggling and mucking around with him made me fall more and more in love. How I wish I were like him with the kids; he would

instantly bring a smile to their faces when he was near them. Always playing and joking around, tickling them or throwing them up in the air if he thought the mood was lowering to just average kid level. I had no idea what a hole would be left in my life, and the kids', without this cheekiness.

When Jock wasn't with us in Rome, we started our days in the same way. Isla and Alfie would sit up at the kitchen table and talk nonstop to Jock on FaceTime about their version of events from the day before and funny things the other one had done. Meanwhile, I made breakfast for them and a coffee for myself. Jock had airfreighted our coffee machine and grinder over. Apparently, this was a critical item we needed as soon as we landed. So he was literally watching over my shoulder as my coffee mentor each morning, telling me to press a button here and tap the milk longer there. Then he'd show me the pouring motion and talk me through how I should pour the milk into the cup in a slow circle.

On this day, before the kids had spoken to Jock, a parcel arrived in the mail. He had sent them a present and they couldn't believe that a package with their names on it could make it all the way to our home in Rome. Jock had given them each a stuffed toy – Piggie and Foxy – sprayed with his aftershave. He also sent them each a pack of cards: one was called 'Emotions' and featured pictures of animals with emotion prompts to help kids build vocabulary for

their 'feelings journey'; the other was called 'Mindful Kids' and contained everyday exercises to help little ones find stillness, confidence and joy in the present moment. They got a book each too, *A Kids Book About Confidence* and *A Kids Book About Empathy*. When they opened the box, Alfie said Papa's smell was in there – Jock's aftershave was a big connection point for him.

While the kids played with their presents, I got to work on breakfast. We are a Weet-Bix family, and I had magically found 'Weetabix' over there. However, there was some pushback from the kids: their palates told them something was slightly different. So there were daily requests for hot breakfasts, which made Jock laugh during our morning FaceTimes. Alfie wanted pancetta and boiled eggs, and Isla wanted scrambled eggs and fresh tomatoes with vinegar and pepper. Alfie wanted warm milk, and Isla wanted me to squeeze her some fresh orange juice. Jock would keep the kids entertained while I began the juggle of getting everything cooked and placed in front of them at the same time. Isla would call out that she was soooo hungry, Alfie would call out and ask how much longer. And Jock would tell them to be kind to their mamma because she was the best mamma they could ever have. It always made me feel really loved and adored when he said things like that to the kids; he was the only person who could give me that type of pat on the back.

In Australia we'd had this chaotic version of breakfast on weekends, but usually Jock was running the kitchen and I was distracting the kids. And just as we would all finish eating, he would start planning with the kids what they wanted to eat for lunch. Food was his love language.

After breakfast on this morning, the kids ran off and played, and Jock and I spoke for another couple of hours. I never enjoyed being apart from Jock; we had rarely spent any nights apart since we had met. But being in Rome setting up our life while he was back in Melbourne made me really sad. I wanted all the firsts to be with him; I wanted the kids' first day at school to be with him, and I wanted him to see the look on Alfie's face when he had his first cacio e pepe in Rome. I remember the conversation this day so well because it was our last one, and also I have Jock's journals now, and he wrote about this conversation too. He wrote that it made him happy to hear that our local cafe in Rome had dropped the price of my coffee to 1 euro, like it charged the locals, and that the lady who owned the wine shop knew my name and had yelled out and waved to me across the street the other day. He felt guilty that he wasn't there to help with the kids, the unpacking, the running around to get bath plugs and tea towels so we could settle in. He felt sad that he couldn't kiss the kids and put them to bed each night. He wrote how proud of me he was, how I was a bit quiet and not quite myself, and how my capability to get through

hard stuff always blew his mind. But overwhelmingly, he was looking forward to being there with us, being part of this adventure, and watching Alfie and Isla become little Aussie Scottish Italian kids.

Our call finished, and we hung up; it was about 6 pm his time back in Melbourne. We texted back and forth for a few hours until midnight his time. When his last text came through, I was cuddled up on the couch with the kids watching *The Lion King*. In the part where Simba's dad died in a stampede, Alfie cringed and curled his face into my chest and said, 'It makes me sad that people don't have a papa.' I didn't text Jock after that as I figured he would be asleep and we'd FaceTime in the morning.

But then, in the morning, Jock missed his usual FaceTime with us. I can't really explain it in words but there was a shift in my universe after he missed the first call. I felt a surge of something go through my body. I tried him again, and when there was no answer, I wrote a list on my phone of things I would need to grab if I urgently had to take the kids to the airport and fly back to Australia: passports, phone, wallet, Isla's blanket, Piggie and Foxy.

I look back at that day now, and there was a final moment in time when, in our hearts and minds, I still had a husband and the children still had a papa. Jock had passed away, but we didn't know yet, and everything in our world was business as usual.

It wasn't until ten very long hours later that I received the phone call I never wanted to get. And then I was running out the door with our little ones back to Australia, heading towards a media storm I had no idea was even happening.

Totally Unprepared

In the hours after I found out Jock was dead, I was in shock but of sound mind, so I started fumbling through the two steps I thought I had to take – first, book our flights from Rome to Melbourne, and second, call the people who needed to know. I had no idea there were infinitely more steps and decisions awaiting me, all of which would have to be made fast.

I wrote a list of people I needed to speak to. The first person was Ava, Jock's 22-year-old daughter. It was really early back in Australia, maybe 5.30 am, when I called her. She didn't answer but called me back a few minutes later. Jock and Ava had a really special relationship; they had been through the wringer a few times together, and year after year they crafted a bigger and more beautiful father–daughter relationship wrapped up in a friendship. I was

telling Ava that she had lost her dad, her best friend and a life of milestones that we had all assumed they would have together. This call made it feel a little bit more real; the reality of the words awakened parts of my brain that knew only complete darkness. I told Ava to call her mum and get her to come over and look after her. Ava said she would, we said we loved each other and I hung up, ending the first phone call. Fuck me, that was not something I ever thought I would need to do, but here I was.

Then I called Jock's parents. He had been estranged from them for years before he died and me calling them would have immediately set off alarm bells, but no one would ever have imagined what those bells' tolling could mean. Then, my brother, Joel. I asked him to speak to my mum, dad and sister for me. Then I called Andy Allen, one of Jock's closest mates and his fellow *MasterChef Australia* judge. He was awake early because he was about to do the show launch interviews with morning radio and TV. He was still at home, so he put me on speaker as I told him and his wife, Alex, that Jock was dead. It was an absolute shock: none of us were crying; we were just speechless. I hadn't called Network 10 yet, so when Andy asked what I wanted him to do, I said he should continue business as usual until I could speak to someone there. This was one of the handful of unreasonable requests I have made of Andy since Jock died, all of which he has said yes to.

Next I called the rest of Jock's best mates, and left messages for a few who were travelling to call me as soon as they got the message. I then contacted Cat Donovan from Network 10; we knew each other professionally and she is a mother and a wife, so I knew she could emotionally hold me in what I was going to tell her. She is also part of the network's senior leadership team, so I felt she would know what to do from there. She took a breath and started speaking to me about what the next few steps might look like. She asked if it was okay for her to call Bev McGarvey, the CEO, to let her know, and for Bev to call me, and I said of course. I have always had a lot of respect for these two women, even more so now.

Bev called me minutes later and, after checking that the kids and I were okay, started talking me through some of the more time-sensitive decisions. She told me that someone was looking into the fastest way to get us home, and not to worry about any of that, as it was in hand. She had also been given my family's contact details and was co-ordinating travel for everyone in the background. I told her I would like to get back to Australia before announcing Jock's death, and she said she didn't feel that would be possible as news like this spread very quickly. I agreed that I would post on his Instagram at a certain time, and Bev advised that they would also prepare a written statement, which she would send to me to review and approve before they published it.

I had naively thought we could fly home, find safety in the arms of family, and then announce that we had lost Jock. But after speaking to Bev I realised I would not have the luxury of that time or privacy to get us home. This news was too big and would naturally find its way out – there would have to be a public announcement. I wrote the statement like I was stuck in an awful, sick dream, in an absolute daze of disbelief and denial:

With completely shattered hearts and without knowing how we can possibly move through life without him, we are devastated to share that Jock passed away yesterday.

So many words can describe him, so many stories can be told, but at this time we're too over-whelmed to put them into words. For those who crossed his path, became his mate, or were lucky enough to be his family, keep this proud Scot in your hearts when you have your next whisky.

We implore you to please let us grieve privately as we find a way to navigate through this and find space on the other side to celebrate our irreplaceable husband, father, brother, son and friend.

We were now hours away from *MasterChef Australia* premiering on TV. Bev suggested they didn't proceed with televising it, but she wanted to know what I wanted – did

I want it to go to air? I said no, and we agreed it wouldn't air for now, and that we would talk more about if and when it would when I arrived in Australia.

I posted the announcement, put my phone on silent and got into an Uber with the kids, our belongings piled on the seats next to us, hastily shoved into plastic bags. We were about to walk back into a life that would never be the same again, as a family that would never be the same.

The Return

We transited through Singapore on our way back to Melbourne, and my sister, Lani, flew over to be with me and help with the kids. When we landed, the crew asked for people to stay seated and they assisted the kids and me off the plane. Both kids were clinging to me; they knew something was terribly wrong because of how upset I had been since we left our home in Rome. I physically didn't think I could make it off the plane, so I prioritised carrying the kids and the crew carried my bags and Isla's pram.

Lani was waiting at the gate, and when I saw her I knew I could let go. I had been holding everything together by frayed threads, and now she was there to take it from me. Only when I saw her did I realise how close I was to collapsing. There was no possible way I could have made it home without her. She took Isla from my arms

and hugged me deeply, with such sadness and care, and we stayed like that for as long as we both needed. Then she jumped into 'Aunty Narni' mode and tried to be upbeat and happy with the kids, telling them she had a surprise that she wanted to give them. She pushed the pram with Alfie in it, Isla clinging on to her chest, and I followed, grateful that another loving adult was present to help care for our little ones as the unbearable truth drew nearer to bursting in on their lives.

I didn't know how to tell the kids; I knew that would be the hardest thing I would ever need to do in my life. Of everything that has happened since Jock died, telling them remains the most heartbreaking part. It was difficult to protect them – Alfie was so excited that we were flying home to Melbourne because he missed his best friend (Jock) and was asking if we could go on a date night (what we call going out for dinner) with Jock when we landed. My face was red and swollen, and I couldn't stop myself from crying, so the kids were worried about me. As we rested in a corner of the lounge in Singapore airport, their gorgeous papa's face was on every TV screen.

That's when I realised this was international news, and we, rather than Jock, were about to become the centre of attention.

As promised, Network 10 had arranged our flights home and when we landed in Melbourne they got us out of the airport without being photographed. Looking

after us was not their responsibility; however, from the moment I called Cat Donovan they looked after us, telling me to just take one step at a time and managing all the unknowns to me that were knowns to them. They understood how the media worked; they knew where we were at risk in both our privacy and safety. I had no idea what I was walking back into, and I definitely had no idea how to find the privacy that we so desperately needed.

We were taken out a side door by security to a convoy of vans where Ava and my family were waiting. Ava stood outside watching for us while everyone else stayed in one of the vans. Seeing her broke my heart. She was destroyed; she had been holding herself together but fell apart when she saw us. The kids were put straight into the van with my family, and Ava and I embraced until we could take a breath and move into the next van. We remained entwined the whole car trip. We physically needed to support each other – the first step in us becoming grief partners through the coming months.

Ava and I hadn't spoken since I called her with the news from Rome so I wanted to bring her up to speed on where everything was at. She is Jock's eldest; if I wasn't married to him she would have been doing all of this. I said with kindness that I would speak to her about everything and I wanted her opinion on everything, but that I would need to be the person to make the final decisions. She understood and accepted that, and in that moment I saw all the

reasons why Jock was so proud of the woman she had become.

We didn't have a home in Australia. We had packed up our life and moved to Rome, so we had no place to go and nothing familiar for the kids. Instead, Network 10 had organised a hotel for us and my family, so we drove there now in the vans that had been sent to meet us. Part of the way in from the airport our van pulled over abruptly on the 100 km/h motorway, as did the one behind us carrying my family and the kids. I was so on edge by that point, the sudden stop threw me completely. Each van had a driver and security person in the front, so I asked what was going on. They explained that the other van had radioed to tell them that Alfie's finger was stuck in something metal down the side of his seat and he was screaming in pain. I needed to get to him – the thought of something happening to one of my children, a part of Jock, blew my mind. I tried to get out to run to their van but we had pulled up against a concrete barrier so I couldn't exit the car. I felt like a caged animal, trying to reach my screaming little boy and being held back by millions of hands. Thankfully, in no time at all, security told me his finger was out and he was calm again, and the vans started moving. I told myself in that moment that I would be within arm's reach of the kids from that point on, that I was all they had left and I had to be nearby in case they needed me.

When we finally arrived in the city centre we were escorted into the hotel, which I have since renamed The Prison. Network 10 had arranged rooms for all of us so we could stay together, and had organised every single thing we might need. The kids' room had play tents set up with toys for each of them, nappies, baby wipes, healthy snacks, bath toys, cute kids' towels with hoods, teddy bears, books, pencils. They had arranged for the bedheads to be removed from the room and the mattresses to be placed next to each other on the floor because they weren't sure if Isla was sleeping in a bed yet or was still in a cot. There was a kitchen too, which was stocked with snacks, soft drinks, wine, fresh fruit. The normal version of me would have felt like this was over the top; I would have texted or called to say thank you and explain how much it meant. But I didn't. I had no capacity for anyone else's feelings; I wasn't thinking about anyone but myself and my children. My brain was so foggy, I had to really concentrate when I was speaking to my family or friends. I was even finding it hard to remember their names off the top of my head.

In retrospect, I respect what my body and mind were gifting me – numbness so I could function, so I could keep moving, albeit at a very slow pace, and continue to be Alfie and Isla's mamma.

We stayed there for maybe seven days, and in that time, the curtains were always drawn. I only got out for fresh air once, when I went to the Coroners Office to see Jock for the

first time. We had photos of Jock printed and put in frames throughout our room, and all Jock's favourite restaurants fed us each day and night. In the safety of The Prison I had no idea what was happening in the media outside those four walls. I had been told it was relentless, but I only know in retrospect that there were thousands of articles being published every day, and that there was a jackpot waiting for the person who could include a photo of Jock's grieving family in their story. I had a moment of realisation when I wanted to get the kids out of our room for a bit and figured the hotel's indoor swimming pool would be a safe zone. However, security advised against the three of us leaving the room, in case someone recognised me and the media were told the name of our hotel.

I was in a media blackout, and I asked that no one talk to me about any story they had read that annoyed or upset them. The TV was to stay off. I only touched my phone if I wanted to call someone, because the quantity of messages and missed calls was extraordinary. Someone else usually had my phone and would answer a call if they thought I would want them to. I got involved when major stories with false information were about to break and I had a chance to combat them, but for the most part, the media machine was so big and so far-reaching, I just had to get out of the way and let it run its course.

Telling the Kids

I didn't have the courage to speak to the kids until the second day in The Prison. My family and some of our close friends sat down for dinner in our room the first night, and I told them I would be telling the kids about it in the morning. I went through how I would like them to behave and how I expected them to mirror my language and behaviour, as this was what I absolutely needed from them. No one was to stray from the path or decide what they thought was best for the kids.

Made-up concepts like 'passed away' and 'heaven' had no meaning for the kids, so I had decided to use very clear words like 'dead' and 'forever'. I would answer any questions with clarity and words that ensured they understood, as best they could, the permanency of this. This directness was critical for the kids to understand

that regardless of how unfair or unbelievable it was, it was forever.

If the kids asked questions I didn't know the answer to, I had decided I would simply say, 'I'm not sure about that.' And if I wasn't ready to answer the question, I would say, 'I'm not sure about that, but I will think about it and let you know.' No matter how hard it was, I was determined to be honest, open and very clear with them, and to check through their body language or words that they understood what I had told them.

I had also decided to tell them the bare minimum. I was going to share the unbearable news in one sentence and leave them space to ponder and ask questions. I was aware that I didn't want to try to substitute myself for Jock with statements like 'But you still have Mamma' because I'm not a replacement for their papa, and it could scare them into thinking something could happen to me at some point too.

The morning I told the kids, I asked that everyone be in our hotel room so it was like the day before, with people around and the sound of voices. I took the kids into my bedroom, got them up onto the bed with me, and with one arm wrapped around each of them, I said, 'I have some very sad news. Papa has died, and he is not coming back.'

After a few seconds, Alfie burst into tears. The kind where he was silent, then the noise came out, then silent before the next wave of pain and sadness could escape.

This triggered Isla – she could tell this was really bad, and she became hysterical. I don't know if I will ever recover from the pain of this moment. There's nothing I wouldn't give for Jock not to have died, but even more, there is nothing I wouldn't give so our little ones didn't have to experience what they were experiencing in that moment. It was despair, absolute despair.

Then I let them have the space to take it in and ask questions. Alfie asked if Papa was ever coming back, and I had to say, 'No, Papa is dead, and that means he can never come back to us. It means we are never able to see him again.' Alfie bargained, 'Not even for a cuddle?', and I responded, 'Papa can never give you cuddles again, darling, because he is dead.'

Alfie then wanted to know where Jock was at that moment. 'Where is Papa right now?' he asked, and I said the doctors had taken him to a place called the Coroners Office.

He misunderstood and said, 'Oh, the doctors are trying to fix him.'

'No, darling, that is where they take people when they die,' I responded.

Alfie then asked what Jock was wearing, and I said he was still wearing his pyjamas. He asked if Jock was in a bed, and I said they had put him in a special box. Alfie asked if Papa would be warm enough, if he had a pillow, and what if he needed to go to the toilet. He asked when

it had happened, and I told him two days ago, that we had started travelling home the moment I found out.

Alfie's next round of questions was more about the loss of his papa. He asked if they could still be best friends, who would do Lego with him, if he was still allowed to cook in Papa's kitchen and if he could still go to *MasterChef*. Then he asked if he could talk to Papa. I said that Papa was dead and he couldn't speak to him anymore, and Alfie said, 'What if I talk, could he still hear me?'

This was when I said, 'I really don't know, darling, but I've been speaking to Papa, and it gives me comfort.'

Isla didn't ask questions; instead she told me her thoughts. Papa is alone, which makes her sad. Papa gets cold quickly, so make sure he isn't cold. Maybe he needs his dressing gown on. She also blamed me; she did this for the next year, and each time, it destroyed me. She said I looked after our family and didn't look after her papa. Why didn't I give him medicine to make him better? Why didn't I call the doctors for Papa? Why wasn't I with him now making him better?

As their questions started to slow down and our crying subsided, I wanted them to understand that this sadness wouldn't go away. So I said that since I had heard Papa had died, I had cried a lot. And in those moments when I cried, sometimes I wanted to be alone, and other times I wanted someone to cuddle me. And with so many people around that love me, love them, love Papa, I always felt

a bit better after one of them cuddled me. I wanted to normalise the feelings the kids would have; they had felt sad before but this wasn't that. This was a sickness, and confusion, and physical ache for their papa, and I didn't want them feeling any of those things and not getting the comfort or nurture they needed. I also didn't want them thinking they had to put words to it, to feel the need to force their broken hearts and minds to explain. I told them that I now had all of Papa's cuddles in my arms, so I had double what I usually did, and anytime day or night they needed cuddles, they just had to come to me.

I asked them what they wanted to do now, and Isla said she wanted to have a cuddle and watch a movie together, so that's what we did. I knew my next step after this was to travel to the Coroners Office to see Jock, so I was taking in the closeness to the kids and allowing my care for them to be my distraction.

I wanted to get them back into their routine as gently but swiftly as I could. I asked if they wanted me to call their old daycare to see if they could both go back there now we were in Melbourne again. They loved that idea, so I messaged and was told, of course, they could come in whatever day worked and for as long as I felt they could handle it. Emma, our old nanny from Melbourne, headed over to be part of their days again. She was more a member of the family than just their nanny, and they received a lot of comfort from her and the normality

of her being back with us again. I tried to pretend that Rome hadn't happened and to get the kids back into their normal Melbourne life, albeit in a hotel room. I set up play dates with Alfie's two best mates from daycare, and my mum and sister took Alfie and Isla to them. I couldn't leave The Prison, but I was also not ready to return to our old life, to do daycare drop-offs, or be in our old park where we had celebrated so many birthdays and Mother's Days.

Very quickly, I saw regression in the kids' behaviour. They were more clingy with me, but also with my mum and sister. They didn't want to eat the things they usually would, they woke constantly during the night like they were newborns and they both started wetting the bed again. Isla also started having night terrors. The changes came almost instantly after I told them about Jock.

The first time they both woke up hysterical in the night, I had to work out which one was my priority; I couldn't comfort them both. Isla was thrashing around, and I knew only I could hold and calm her down. So I reached out and held Alfie's hand while I cradled Isla in my arms and rocked her gently. After this, my mum and sister stepped in as co-parents. They have always been very respectful of me as a mum, never saying I should do this or that or moving into a space when I'm trying to do something, but they could both see what I was facing and sense that the kids needed them more than ever.

So one of them would come into the dark room and cuddle the one I couldn't hold.

Alfie has had to have more independence throughout his regression. Isla was only two years old, still so little, when Jock died, so I gravitated to her needs and tried to give Alfie the comfort I could through holding his hand and using my words. I worry about the impact of this in the longer term. I see his behaviour even now: if Isla cries, he finds a solution to calm her, and most of the time, he gives up something or is worse off.

Learning to be a solo parent was draining but also heartbreaking in that I knew I couldn't meet either of my children's emotional needs fully. They expected me to split my attention and my touch equally at all times. When we sat down to eat a meal, I had to sit in between them. If one of them held my hand, the other would hold my hand too. If I was tickling Isla's back, Alfie would sidle up and want his back tickled at the same time. I literally couldn't get anything done when the kids were with me. They wanted all of my attention: I couldn't read a text because they talked at me to prevent me from reading it; they were quiet in the car but as soon as someone called and I answered, the kids wouldn't stop screaming out or singing. They wanted every ounce of me, and my tank was so depleted I went into another layer of despair and guilt over what I saw as my inability to be the mother they needed, the mother Jock's children deserved.

Saying Goodbye

After telling the kids, I wanted to see Jock as soon as I could, so I was taken to him the morning after we landed. I hadn't even been to bed the night before, I just walked around the hotel room in a daze. Time had no relevance; I felt neither awake nor tired. I looked out at all the lights on the streets and at the highrise buildings of the city and I wished I was one of those people, carefree and going about life like nothing had happened.

It was a tricky operation to get Ava and me in to see Jock at the Coroners Office. Security had worked out a strategy, and we were taken down in a service elevator, through the back corridors of the hotel and into a van in the loading dock. I had asked Joey, one of my friends, and my brother, Joel, to come with us as I figured Ava and I might literally need support. Joel was my go-to and Joey

was Ava's. At the Coroners Office carpark the van pulled in behind a wall and we braced ourselves for going inside.

The others got out of the car, but I needed a moment to compose myself. I was physically overwhelmed by the thought of what was about to unfold. There were so many moments of disbelief and in this one I couldn't manage to catch my breath. I realised later this was the beginning of the panic attacks that would leave me feeling weak and incapable, and usually angry at myself.

Sitting in the back of the van, I felt paralysed. I was getting myself ready to see my gorgeous husband, dead, completely defenceless, robbed of life, there but not with us.

Would it be like he was sleeping? Would he look peaceful? Could I read his face and know what had happened? Jock and I were always connected, and I still felt it. When he didn't answer my call there was a tilt in my universe that made everything fall into dysfunction. My therapist likened it to a baby's mobile hanging over a cot: when one of the four hanging toys breaks off, the balance is gone and it folds into itself.

Joel waited for me a few metres away, a polite but protective distance. I took a deep breath and climbed out of the van. He asked if I was okay. I gave him a nod, then he wrapped an arm around my shoulder and we started to walk towards the door.

When we entered the building we were met by a man who gently directed us to a room with a small seating area.

He spoke softly and slowly. He was all I could handle outside of our immediate circle of friends and family who were staying in The Prison with us. He had the delicate task of acting as the official conduit between us and the Coroner, who was reviewing Jock's case in the Coroners Court up the hallway. We sat down and the softly spoken man told us that Jock was in the next room. Ava and I couldn't stop crying. Jock was literally metres away from us, but we couldn't be further apart – 'so close but so far' had never been truer.

First there was admin to be done: I signed some paperwork and there was a little back and forth with the Coroner. Then the softly spoken man explained what would happen next – he indicated a door and told us that Jock was just on the other side of it and we would see him as soon as the door was opened. He was lying with a sheet up to his chin and he was still dressed in the pyjamas he had on when they brought him in. The man explained that there was a glass wall between where we would enter and where Jock was; if we wanted them to retract the wall so we could be closer to Jock, he could do that for us. He told us that we could touch Jock, and not to be alarmed by how cold he was. As we were about to enter he reassured us that we could stay for as long as we wanted, it was up to us.

Ava and I both nodded our heads and then, somehow, I was standing looking at my gorgeous husband. At this point, I was just going in with Ava to help acclimatise

her to the room and to seeing Jock, then I'd leave her for however long she needed. Seeing Jock in that moment, my heart completely broke, and I doubt it will ever recover. This was real. I hadn't seen Jock, hadn't touched him, since we said goodbye at the airport weeks before. I asked Ava if she was ready for me to leave, she nodded and I walked out.

As I came back through the door, Joel pounced out of his seat and held me without talking, without pity. I sobbed into my big brother's shoulder, but any noise was drowned out by Ava's cries on the other side of the wall. She was in so much pain. It was the sound of profound loss, of feeling the depth of life's suffering. She was being dragged through the awful experience of losing a parent decades before she was meant to. This was unfair for all of Jock's children, but there was an extra sting for Ava as the adult child, the one who first made him a dad, the one who had a deep friendship with him. Ava deserved the opposite. But like she always has, she put one foot in front of the other and copped the waves trying to take her footing.

When Ava came out of the room, I gave her an enormous hug, but I knew with deep sadness that nothing anyone could do was going to make her feel even marginally better. We were grief partners. I hadn't put the name to it yet, but we were in this together; we were the only two who had a similar grief fingerprint. I handed her over to Joey, took a breath and walked in to say my goodbye to Jock.

My love was now lying alone in front of me. I stood next to him, looking down at a picture from my worst nightmare, trying to work out how to start my goodbye. I moved to Jock's head to look down at his face. The face I had gazed at millions of times. I knew the shape of his lips, the touch of his cheek, his eyes, every laughter line from the thousands of mornings I had woken up next to him; I knew his hairline from running my fingers through his hair every day we were together. That is who was now lying alone in front of me. I hadn't seen a dead body before. It shouldn't have been my husband, the father of our two- and five-year-old children. I was hysterical for a while.

I told myself he was just sleeping. I'm not sure if this was a mistake because even now, writing this, Jock being dead isn't a real thing that I have accepted. I wanted to touch him, but I was scared. I was scared of the coldness. I started by touching his hair, stroking his hair back like I had done so many times before. He smelt like Jock; I could smell his aftershave, the de-curling stuff he put through his hair. There was a chemical smell in the room, but I knew his smell and I focused on that. I built up the courage to touch his forehead, then his cheek, and then I stopped crying and started talking to him in a low voice.

'What the fuck happened? Where are you? Is this real?'

I cried quiet tears on him, my tears landing on his face. I told him that I would make sure the kids had happy and

whole lives, that I would be okay, that I had this – all the things he would've known already. I tried to describe my love for him, as I had so many times before, but it felt like being in one of those olden-day movies when someone's getting on a train and needs to profess their undying love in a millisecond. I was trying to say my last goodbye, give my last kiss goodnight.

I kissed his forehead. I kissed his cheeks. I rested my cheek against his, my hand behind his neck, savouring what had been such a basic daily occurrence, and now was the last. I knew this was the closest to him I would ever be again. I felt he was still there, that the spirit of Jock was behind those eyes and wanting to say so many things, but death stifled them.

As I cried over his face, my tears pooled around his left eye and I looked at him, wondering how he could feel so real to me, but be gone. I kept telling him to wake up. I pleaded with him to open his eyes, just gift me one last moment of connection with him. And then a tear ran down the side of his face. One of my tears had been released from the pool around his eye and fell down his cheek to his ear like it was his own; it looked like he was crying. I didn't wipe the tear away, I left a part of me with him forever. Much later, this deep moment of grief gave me joy, in that a part of me was with him.

I tried to say goodbye so many times, but I just couldn't leave him. Seeing his face gave me calmness. It gave me the

strength that I needed to carry on. It was the tiniest seed of strength but it would grow from there.

It took everything I had to leave him. Walking away from Jock lying there in that room felt like the end. It was my last moment to see his face, to touch him, to talk to him, to just have him close. It was one of the hardest things I have had to do since losing him.

Love at First Sight

I grew up in the suburbs of Sydney with an older brother and sister. We felt like an average family, but considering the salaries of a pilot and a school teacher, I realise we lived a reasonably affluent life. We had trips to Disneyland, street food in Bangkok, banana pancakes on the beach in Phuket, and onion rings in Hawaii.

Dad being a pilot was challenging – he was away for large chunks of time when we were little, sometimes for more than fourteen days. So we had a life with Mum, which was reasonably independent and semi-supervised, but which turned into a dictatorship when Captain Jack walked back into the house. From a young age, I learnt to read situations, get what I needed from them, and talk my way out of trouble.

As an adult, that made me a highly competitive person, a perfectionist, and someone who liked everything to be in order and planned. I started my marketing and advertising agency when I was 23 years old, and used those skills to lead both my business and my life in general. As the years passed, as friendships and relationships fell to the side, as my staff kept leaving, I realised there was a flaw in my strategy.

I set about trying to understand my behaviour in order to be a better and genuinely happier version of myself. At first I thought I could read lots of books, that that would iron things out for me. But this led me down side streets as I tried to understand the people closest to me and the impact we had on each other. I read books on the significance of birth order in a family. I read about trauma and its effects on happiness. This led to a deep dive into books about addiction, a subject I felt drawn to given my childhood with a dad who drank heavily and constantly. I found Tanya, a therapist who had done a lot of work in addiction, and my weekly sessions with her began.

My dad is a hard man, and years of living with his emotional and physical abuse through childhood and adulthood were catching up to me. I didn't want to think or behave like him, with his alcohol addiction underpinning his personality and actions and allowing him to forget his meanness and the beltings he would give us. I always seemed to get more beltings than my brother and sister,

which evolved from hand to wooden spoon to leather belt. I had a childhood of being absolutely terrified of my dad, never feeling any closeness or safety with him.

The physical abuse stopped when I was maybe six or seven, when Joel, who was only 18 months older than me, told my dad he was never to touch me again. Tanya worked with me on unpacking that, on understanding addiction and addictive personalities, and we landed very quickly on the finding that I was, in fact, nothing like my dad. I have done a lot of work on this, and I think it was my deep knowledge of addiction that allowed me to understand and accept Jock when he came into my life.

I had been single for a couple of years when I met Jock. One of my friends, Jo-Ellen, had met him at an event, and she said he was the ultimate match for me. She said he was a chef, a champagne ambassador, and European. When she had called to tell me this, I was in Paris. She sent me some photos from the event, and a screenshot of his Instagram. Zonfrillo was a unique name. There he was in a slim-fitting three-piece suit, curly hair, mouth wide open, laughing, looking smoking hot. When I found out his European type was Scottish, I have to admit I was disappointed. I mean, technically, he's from Europe, but I had assumed he would be some smooth French or Spanish version. Little did I know then how much this Scottish-Italian mongrel would fit me.

Jock has told the story of how we met in so many interviews over the years. I fear I'm wasting space in this book writing about it again. I'll do the short version. After I had assumed Jo-Ellen would magically hook me up with this chef she barely knew, he left my mind. Months later I was at my sister Lani's house for Joel's birthday, and it was over that dinner I told my family I had given up on dating and men.

The dinner finished late, and it would take me close to an hour to get home, so I jumped in an Uber and started responding to missed text messages and clearing out bad photos on my phone. Midway through selecting photos for deletion, I came across the screenshot of Jock's Instagram page. He was still very hot. I then went into my emails, and saw a Twitter notification about some new followers, and Jock was one of them. Beauty. So I sent him a message and while I was still in the Uber he replied. This continued for a few hours, and then in the early hours of Sunday morning we moved to texting and kept messaging until I had to leave at 8 am for a class at the gym with some friends.

I've always believed in a big love. One that would change the course of my life, take me somewhere that just kept evolving and blossoming into something more fulfilling and meaningful as the years rolled by. Some friends warned me that I was being unrealistic and setting myself up for a life alone. But it was now Sunday morning and the

direction of my life had started to shift, though I had no idea this was occuring – until Tuesday, when Jock arrived in Sydney to take me out for dinner. We locked eyes for the first time, and it was love at first sight.

It took mere days for Jock to tell me he loved me, and we started planning life together. I had booked in to have my eggs frozen the coming January, and when I told Jock this he asked why I didn't just go off the pill so we could start trying for a baby. I had never really thought about having children; I was just freezing my eggs as a safety net, but with Jock I wanted everything, and I wanted it immediately. The babymaking began two months into our relationship, and four months after that we bought a house together in the Adelaide Hills, three months after that we were engaged, six months after that we were married, and six months after that we had done a successful round of IVF, after trying for a year and a half to fall pregnant naturally, and I was pregnant with our first little baby, Alfie.

Alfie's entry into the world was a scary one. Jock and I had gone to Italy for a couple of weeks as he was cooking at some events there. I then flew back to Adelaide and he went to the Faroe Islands to film a TV show. We never did this – Jock had flown me home to Australia and then returned to Europe a couple of times during our life together, but on this occasion we were jamming things in before Alfie was born, so we agreed we would divide

and conquer. A day after I arrived home, I went in for a scheduled check-up with Sabrina, a friend who was also my obstetrician. I drove home and was unpacking my suitcase from Italy when she called and said I would need to come back in. She had reviewed my tests and it looked like Alfie needed to be born in the next 24 hours.

Prior to me falling pregnant, my doctor had identified an issue with the shape of my uterus and thought this could be the reason I was unable to fall pregnant naturally. Once IVF was successful, they kept a close eye on it. Now, during my regular scan, it looked like an area of my uterus wasn't showing blood flow or allowing Alfie to grow into that space. They also saw an irregular and weak flow through my umbilical cord, meaning that at any point the flow might not be strong enough to pump oxygen and nutrients through to Alfie.

I tried to negotiate with Sabrina; I asked if I could sleep at home that night and head in tomorrow, but she said no, I should pack my bags and calmly make my way to the hospital.

This wasn't meant to be happening. I wasn't meant to have my baby for two and a half months. And when I did, Jock was definitely not meant to be on a tiny island near Iceland.

Jock had no phone coverage, so I was only able to communicate with him when he returned to his hotel each night. As it was now morning where he was, he would have

already left for a long day of filming. I rebooked his flights so he could be on the next plane out of there, messaged him and also left a message at his hotel to explain what had happened, then I packed my hospital bag. Before I got in the car to drive to the hospital, I walked into our baby's room and it was empty. We had bought some bits and pieces, and I had bought a pram, but we didn't have a cot or any clothing or supplies. I realised we would never have the joy of setting up our baby's room together, and this was the beginning of many firsts we weren't able to have with Alfie.

Once I arrived at the hospital Sabrina took me to the maternity ward, where I was strapped into scanners so they could constantly monitor Alfie's heartbeat and the flow of oxygen through my umbilical cord. This was when the hourly decision about whether Alfie was being born commenced. If Sabrina wasn't happy with the flow, it could mean Alfie was being starved of oxygen, and he needed to come out straight away. I was trying not to think about going into the birthing suite without Jock; I couldn't comprehend the impact that would have on me, and also on him. By this point it was quite late at night, but day and night had no relevance there, so one of the paediatric doctors came and took me for a walk through the NICU (neonatal intensive care unit). He wanted to acclimatise me to where I would be spending the coming months, and to show me the size of the babies who were

in there so I was better prepared to see Alfie. There was no joy in that room; sadness and worry hung in the air, and there was hardly any baby noise or people talking.

I returned to my room and tried to will the universe to keep Alfie inside me until Jock was by my side. First thing in the morning my family arrived on flights from Sydney, and we all just sat wondering what time I would be wheeled in to have our little baby boy. The day passed and there were now only a few hours till Jock landed back in Adelaide. I told my family it was all good and they could head home, and I waited for Jock. He landed and called me straight away; he said he would run to a taxi and leave his bags behind. He arrived at the hospital carrying two bags of Oporto with him. I couldn't believe it – he was in such a rush he'd left his suitcases going round and round on the baggage carousel, but he'd taken the time to have his taxi go through a drive-through to buy some burgers and fries for us. I'm happy I didn't get too angry at him because it ended up being another two weeks before Alfie was born.

Our gorgeous tiny baby was a wee 1.2 kgs when he arrived, and after a few seconds on my chest, he was taken away by the specialist team. As we'd agreed, Jock left me and stayed with Alfie every second. That is when their deep bond started, when Jock felt completely responsible for caring for our little boy.

The next morning Ava arrived from Sydney to see her baby brother. She sat with him all day, her hand through

the side of his humidicrib, one finger stroking his small body and face. Jock spoke to me and said that if Alfie was allowed to come out of his humidicrib that day for a cuddle, could Ava be the one to cuddle him, just in case Alfie didn't make it. He was allowed out for a brief moment, and Ava got her first cuddle with her brother.

I didn't get to hold Alfie again for two days, and Jock had to wait even longer. Given where our life is now, after losing Jock, I am that extra bit prouder of Alfie's endurance. In moments when Jock questioned if Alfie would make it, if we would ever bring our little boy home, I would just look into Alfie's eyes – we had an unspoken agreement that everything would be okay. He gives me that strength now.

Jock imagined the worst – he was a worrier, and if the worst didn't happen he felt like it was a win. Each day he spent falling in love with Alfie, watching me as a mamma for the first time, and watching Alfie and me fall more deeply in love, made him fear the awful outcome even more. The awful outcome never came, but it left a deep scar on Jock that he never recovered from and was only able to explain to me through his therapy years later. It was a period in Jock's life when he realised he wasn't invincible and that really bad stuff could happen.

Our beautiful Isla was born two and a half years later and our family was complete. She was three times the size of Alfie, and after she was born she was put on my chest

and started to feed. I couldn't believe I was able to hold her for so long without someone taking her from me. After six hours of having her on my chest, Jock asked if he could have a cuddle, and I reluctantly handed her over. He had already asked the kitchen to cook him a steak and fries, accompanied by a glass of red wine, so he was ready to settle in for a night of Isla cuddles. Many nights when we were home I would look at the baby monitor to check on the kids and find Jock in Isla's cot with her. Literally curled up in there with her. He didn't go in because she was crying – he went in because he missed her when she was sleeping.

Life with Jock was vibrant, exciting and filled with adventure. Of course there were also the ragged edges of life catching up with him and trying to deal with the past. Jock and I understood each other in a way that is hard to put into words. I don't doubt that he was the person the universe gifted me, and somehow we found our way to each other. It was not all rosy and perfect – we had really big and hard conversations, we disagreed, I held up a mirror to some of his behaviours and mindsets and told him he needed to try harder even though trauma was the root cause. I knew how to make him a better version of himself, the version he was really trying to be. I knew how to forgive and how to push, always loyal and always his person.

We agreed that life would be a sprint so we could sit back and enjoy an early retirement, a life somewhere in Italy. In saying that, we didn't give anything up for that life. Our

life was epic. We were smug. Or maybe only I was smug; Jock was forever the pessimist, and I tried so hard to iron that crease out of his thinking.

During our last Italian summer together, we spent nine weeks travelling with the kids. Partway through that trip we started writing down potential pathways to an Italian life. It went from staying in a cheap little 'bothy' somewhere, to living in a capital city so the kids could attend international schools and Jock could fly in and out for work more easily. When we started to talk through the range of options, we kept gravitating to the more extreme end, which was living in Italy permanently. It didn't scare us. It felt inevitable. So the move-to-Rome master plan was formed, research began, and visa and passport applications commenced.

My fit with Jock was beyond anything I can even comprehend now. I knew every day we were together that we were fucking great, but I know it even more now. I just really enjoyed being around him. On the weekends Jock would let me sleep in and then bring me coffee in bed. When I was ready to start moving, I'd head downstairs and find him dishevelled in the kitchen, his thick, curly hair going crazy without any product in it to hold it down; he would have Alfie up on his cooking stool with a skewer and a pile of crepes, and Jamie Oliver's butterscotch sauce simmering away on the stove. Jock was at his happiest on weekend mornings – he would put on his

Scottish playlist, and the kids would know it was breakfast when they heard bagpipes. We would wander around the house all day in our dressing gowns. Nothing mattered to Jock on the weekends except being in the kitchen and teaching Alfie how to cook, guiding his hands, showing him what signs to look for before he could turn the crepe. My boys. My extraordinary life.

When Jock packed up the house for Rome, we sent some boxes airfreight as they were so urgent we couldn't live without them for more than a week. His crepe pan and Alfie's cooking stool were in there along with our coffee machine, grinder and every sized Microplane we owned. None of our shoes were urgent, apparently, but boy could we cook lots of crepes.

Our little family was Jock's absolute world; it was like the kids and I were his docking station where he felt safe and understood, and charged back up to get out there. He used a loud, sweary voice, tattoos and whisky drinking to seem invincible, but it was all just a distraction. And I have to admit that sometimes I got distracted by that too and fell into letting him be the strong one for me, for us. So to enter the chaos of grief without him felt like starting below zero, and the work I had to do just to get back to the starting line was immense.

Chef in Shining Armour

After saying my goodbye to Jock at the Coroners Office, I returned to The Prison to meet with the detectives who were working on Jock's case. They were calm and respectful, and told me this was just a routine visit. They informed me they had watched all the CCTV footage from when Jock had checked in to the hotel to when the police did their welfare check; they had spoken to staff, inspected his room and gone through his bags, his journals, his notebooks, and their finding was that he had died of natural causes.

They compassionately explained the scene for me from when they entered his room. They said it looked as you'd expect a hotel room to look, some dirty clothes on the floor, but very peaceful, and that Jock was simply lying in bed under the covers sleeping. They said he had fallen asleep with his phone in his hand. His last message had

been to me and I hadn't responded. I imagine he had his phone in his hand waiting for my reply to come through before he went to sleep.

As soon as our meeting finished, I was handed a catalogue of coffins. I needed to choose one. I couldn't let my eyes even look at a picture of a coffin, so I told Joey and my friend JT to choose a dark one with nice handles, trusting whatever they thought was best.

In a matter of six hours, I had held my little ones close while I told them their papa was forever gone. I had seen my husband and run my fingers through his hair like I had every day since we met. I had sat down with the detectives who had found Jock. And I had agreed on a coffin for Jock's body. I had nothing left to give and I was only 1 per cent of the way through what needed to be done. Thankfully Andy and Alex, the two people the kids and I needed to be there in that moment, had arrived.

Jock and Andy had been through a lot together. They were two very different men who found common ground in every aspect of their lives. Andy had been a part of our life as a family pretty much every day. He would join our daily FaceTime chats with Jock each morning when he was making coffees and getting his hair and makeup done at the *MasterChef* studio, along with Maureen (Maurzy) and Charmaine (Charz), who worked on the show too. These three friends came into my life because

of *MasterChef* and Jock, and have been so important to me since Jock died.

When we hung out, it was always the four of us – Andy, Alex, Jock and me. The friendship outside of that sat with the boys – they made the plans, and Alex and I happily went along with them. We did everything from dining in Michelin-starred restaurants to making cacciatore and reorganising and labelling containers in our pantry for an afternoon. Being together was really simple and always involved delicious food, natural wine, and anchovies. We enjoyed being in each other's homes; that was where we would spend most of our time together. Ava has a friendship with Andy and Alex too, and Alfie and Isla love them.

Getting Andy and Alex into The Prison to see the kids and me was close to mission impossible. I think this was the beginning of Andy stepping into a new space for the kids and me – it was like he had made an unspoken commitment to Jock that he was going to be there for us, our safety net. Media surrounded their house, and it looked like we simply wouldn't be able to be together. The route that was eventually mapped out for them to get to us was ridiculous and actually unfair for two people who had just lost a close friend. They must have had no energy for this, but somehow they found it so we could see them and still protect our privacy. I was with the detectives when Andy and Alex eventually arrived in our hotel room.

They instantly set to work and started unpacking days and days' worth of the kids' and my favourite meals, which they had both been preparing and labelling for us.

When I finished meeting with the detectives, I walked into the kitchen, and the two people I needed most were there for me. It was so awful for us all, but we had the privacy of the kitchen in which to take our moment. The three of us embraced: Andy and I were hugging, Alex had her arms around both of us. There's no such thing as an awkwardly long cuddle at a time like this; who will ever know how long it went for.

Eventually, our tears stopped, and Andy said he had started dinner for us. He made vodka pasta for the kids; it was their favourite and they ate it whenever we went out for dinner with Andy and Alex. He admitted that making the sauce for the kids was one of the most nerve-racking things he'd had to do. He didn't want to mess up the sauteed onions because he was certain Alfie would taste if they were browned rather than translucent. He served up big bowls of pasta, and it was devoured – the kids ate more than they had in days. For many days afterwards, they had vodka pasta sauce, sausage rolls, brownies and roast chicken, all of which were now stocked up in our fridge, courtesy of the Allens.

Andy and Alex made a big spread for the adults' dinner. Roast chook, roast potatoes, a pumpkin salad, beans and some other healthy options. As they were preparing dinner,

I put the kids to bed. Before long they both woke up crying hysterically. They were merely hours into trying to digest that Papa was not coming back and their little minds couldn't rest. I stayed with them, trying to calm them down and resettle them, but I just couldn't get either of them to take a big breath or even get close to dozing back off. When I re-emerged from their room, easily half an hour or so later, Andy and Alex's beautiful home-cooked meal was sitting cold on the table, with everyone politely waiting for me so that we could start eating dinner together. This was the first of weeks and weeks of cold meals and cold coffees. Something kept coming up that would pull me away, and I felt like the universe wasn't ready for me to enjoy food without Jock.

Bev and Cat from Network 10 were in constant contact during that time. I don't know how they were able to mirror my emotional state but they knew when to contact me, what tone of voice to use, what I was able to handle. In the first couple of days, Bev might call me four times a day, then as time went on she would call or text. Cat was the same. It's hard to explain the variations of what I could handle, and speaking to anyone at all usually meant they would tell me something had gone wrong or needed to be fixed.

Bev and Cat were both keeping me up to speed on anything critical, checking how the kids and I were and organising absolutely anything we needed, from medical

support from a psychiatrist and a doctor, to around-the-clock security, transport so Ava could get some fresh air and go for a walk far away from our hotel, or food supplies, and bath toys for the kids.

When we had settled into The Prison, Bev had called to discuss her idea to film a tribute show for Jock with some of those closest to him; she wanted to see how I felt about that. I thought it was a beautiful idea, and I knew that Bev and Cat were the right people to lead that for him, and for us. It would be ideal to air it that coming weekend, which was a few days away, so I wrote a list of the people I thought could honour Jock, and then left it to them from there.

Andy was, of course, part of the tribute show and was filming the next morning, so he and Alex left. It was going to be beyond overwhelming for him: it had only been a couple of days and now he was walking back into the *MasterChef* kitchen to talk about Jock. In retrospect, I realise what a cruel request to make of him this was, but he did it. He would've done anything for me, and I know that is indefinite and infinite.

It felt like a vacuum when Andy and Alex left; a shift as energy that I really needed disappeared. We didn't know when we would be able to see each other again – the media attention on their house wasn't dying down, and Andy was adamant that he wasn't going to risk the kids' and my privacy if they were followed. Andy and Alex both checked

in on me across the days; someone would see their name come up on my phone and always make sure the phone was answered and given to me wherever I was.

Alex had thoughtfully left Ava and me each a bag of things we didn't know we needed – fluffy dressing gowns, house socks, satin pillowcases, small packets of tissues, lavender sleep spray for our pillows, eye drops. This was the beginning of Alex caring for me, of us creating our own friendship that was not wrapped up with the boys. We have spent more time together since Jock died than we had in the years before, and she is now one of my closest and most loyal friends – someone I am so grateful to have in my life.

Spirituality

I wouldn't say I'd ever been a spiritual person before losing Jock, although I've always been pretty fluid about what I believe the universe is up to. Now, in the new version of me, I have fallen into being a deeply spiritual person. I've noticed this is growing, not diminishing, as the months pass by. I find myself defending this spirituality – giving people a little warning before I start explaining – so they don't think grief has sent me insane. I need to stop that.

I can break my newfound spirituality into stages. I have been realising it in pieces, and now I've settled on what I think it will look like for me for the rest of my life. I am grateful for the belief I have in something that is beyond the people walking around me each day. I truly believe that each person in this world has impact and belonging, and when they are loved and there is

connection they can't just disappear from the world. I am not religious, and allowing my mind to be spiritual has given me a perspective that I initially worried was a coping mechanism. I was concerned that it was my mind gifting me a make-believe world that I could retreat into and still have Jock with me. But then I realised that I didn't care if that was what it was; I believed it to be true. It gave me comfort in some dark and lonely moments that no one could bring me through but myself, and I see proof of it being real constantly.

It started when I lost Jock. In that moment when he didn't answer my first FaceTime call, I knew he was dead. That is wildly dramatic; there's no reason I would think that was why he didn't answer his phone. He could have just been in the bathroom or on another call. But I felt something shift, and I knew he wasn't there anymore and that my world would never be the same again. I think he was already trying to communicate with me; he was inside my head, willing me to follow my gut and find him. I read about Jock's perspective on death in an interview he did years ago, where he said, 'I have seen a lot of ghosts, so I don't know what it is, I think there is something after we die.'

I then saw the spirituality in our little ones, who were innocently folding it into their lives without even knowing or questioning what it was. Initially, it was at night, when their minds were calm and when Jock would normally be

reading them books and putting them to bed. One of the first nights back in Australia, Alfie told me, 'When I get into bed, Papa just flies around and around up there.' I asked him what he meant because I hadn't used the concept of heaven or anything like 'Papa is looking down on you'. He replied like I was an idiot, 'Up there, Mamma, why can't you see him? He's just near the light, talking to us.' Then he started putting his fingers in circles like he was making his own binoculars and said, 'Just use these if you can't see him, Mamma.'

Another night, the kids were talking after I had put them to bed, so I went in to ask what was going on. They both had their hands in the air, making a circle with their fingers and palms; they said Papa wanted more kisses, and they had to send them to him through the tunnel. That is absolutely something Jock would tell them to do.

I immediately began searching for books that might help the kids to understand, that might give them comfort, but that would also give me the words to explain what was happening and what they were feeling. Some books I bought, others my friends found for us, but the one that has become part of our vocabulary is *The Invisible String*. It explains that even if someone who loves you isn't physically with you – which could be because of death or just being separated on your first day at school – there is always an invisible string from their heart to yours. That landed for the kids. They use the idea when one of them is upset,

or if I am going to do something by myself – they tell me it's okay because their invisible string is connected to me.

I feel the truth of this too: Jock and I are still connected. I see him in nature and in wildlife, and I feel him with me in nearly every moment. When I sit out at his grave, I put one of my hands on the grass where his heart would be, I close my eyes and I can feel movement or a shift in the light around me. I say, 'Where are you, Jock? Come back to us,' and he just apologises to me.

I began talking to Jock after we had buried him. I think I felt he was at rest and in his forever place, and now we would find our new rhythm. I haven't shared with more than a couple of people that I talk to Jock – both in my head and out loud – because, again, I don't want people thinking grief has made me insane. But no day goes by that this doesn't happen. Actually, not many hours go by when I'm not communicating with him in some way – from the simple moments like when Isla's body language drops into shrugging her shoulders and using her hands like a little Italian, and I say to him, 'Ha, look at your little girl,' through to stressful moments, when I ask him, 'Jock, what the fuck should I do?'

On the day of Jock's funeral, as I was leaving the cemetery I noticed two kookaburras sitting on a headstone with BARRY written on it in big, bold letters. Barry is the name Jock was born with, and he thought kookaburras were the most exquisite bird (I think they might be one

of the only animals he hadn't eaten). I have since driven the same way out of the cemetery many times and never found that headstone again. And now, every time I visit Jock, a kookaburra flies in within minutes and sits with me. When the kids spend time out with Jock, it is their job to water his grass, fertilise it and also cut it if it gets too long. When they walk over to the tap to fill up their little watering cans, they're out of my sight, so the kookaburra flies over with them and sits in the tree next to the tap, only a metre or two out of reach of the kids, then flies back when they start walking back. The bird is not scared of us, it's drawn to us.

I feel Jock in rainbows. In moments of sadness or deep gratitude, I often see a rainbow. Alfie also told me one day that rainbows make him think of Papa, as has my mum, and only last week my sister told me of times she felt Jock was there with her when she saw a rainbow. Rainbows were never something Jock talked about or said he loved, but somehow we individually feel him in them.

About eight months after losing Jock, I felt like he had left me. I didn't feel his presence, I didn't hear his voice in my head and I figured it was over. I wasn't sure if it was that he wanted me to get on with life and to let him go, or if I had moved on and needed to let him go. Then we had Christmas, and I felt nothing from him. I was up until the early hours of Christmas Eve, wrapping presents by myself, speaking out loud to him, and getting

nothing back. Then, a week later, I felt his shadow next to me, and we had a full conversation. He said he was sorry that he had left me to deal with all of this, that he was sad I had to put on a happy face and get the kids through their first Christmas without him, and he kept telling me how upset he was at missing out. I told him it was not his fault, it's just where our life landed, and he kept apologising.

The final faith point for me is our little ones knowing things that I have never told them, that only Jock could have told them somehow. I had a conversation with Jock about something only he could know, then the next morning, Isla said the exact same thing to me, explaining that Papa had told her. I know she is speaking her truth, and I'm not scared by it – I want to nurture that in the kids. I want them to know I believe them, to keep telling me these things, and I want to understand their experiences with spirituality.

Alfie has a spiritual connection with his papa too, as I realised when we had a conversation that was impossible to dream up. I hadn't taken Alfie to the Coroners Office with me to see Jock – this is one 'forever' decision I have mulled over a lot. I felt Jock wanted me to, but my gut told me it was way too risky at the time. How would a five-year-old handle that? I didn't even know how I was going to handle it. I have since spoken about this with Jock; I have apologised and said I couldn't see how Alfie would benefit from it and that taking Alfie there would have been

more for Jock to say goodbye to his best mate. I saw Jock a few times before we buried him. The first time, at the Coroners Office, I felt his presence; his spirit was still there, and it really was like he was just peacefully sleeping. The following times, it didn't feel like him anymore. Then Alfie told me one morning, 'Mamma, you should have taken me to see Papa and say goodbye. Just the first time because he was still in there; the other times, he wasn't there anymore.' I have never told the kids that I went to see Jock; Alfie doesn't even understand the concept of seeing someone when they have died. The only answer that I believe in is that Jock had been speaking to him.

When these moments come along – and they do regularly – I get a calmness from them, knowing that Jock hasn't just disappeared from this world and that when I need him in my thoughts, he is there. But more importantly, I know that his connection with our little ones extends beyond gifts and treats; his presence and being are embedded in them. They are forever connected, and through spirituality the kids and I still get Jock to ourselves. So I will nurture that spirituality and access to him as they grow older because I too am living with him through mine.

The Politics of Death

Every family has its politics, legacy arguments that are never resolved and grudges whose origins you can't remember. Jock left behind two daughters, one from each of his ex-wives, and parents in Scotland who he had been estranged from for years leading up to his death.

I spoke to Ava and said I was open to her input; however, I would be making any final decisions. It was an important step when so many decisions needed to be made, and some of them required instant action. I am also the person who knows the real Jock best.

I found quite a few interactions with people over the weeks following Jock's death astounding. It wasn't just that they were absolutely disrespectful, but more than that, I couldn't believe their insensitivity. The number of people who were trying to get into Jock's funeral created an

enormous admin task in itself. One of his friends, who I had never heard of, forwarded the funeral invitation to me and said she and her boyfriend would be attending. I kindly explained it was by invitation only, and the invitation she had was addressed to her ex-husband and not to her. She responded by saying she had known Jock for years and had every right to be there, and that she had also spoken to one of Jock's ex-wives, who said she should be allowed to attend. Another person said they had known Jock longer than me, so they should be allowed to attend. And another old friend of Jock's emailed me and said they had spoken to the 'event organisers' and been told they could attend.

I then had to deal with Marco, the guy we had rented the apartment from in Rome, after finding out he had put our apartment on Airbnb. We had paid six months' rent in advance, our possessions were in there, and he was renting it out on Airbnb – it blew my mind. The part that upset me the most was that all of Jock's belongings were there, potentially being used without any care. They were the last parts I had of him, and all I could picture was the chef's knives that he so meticulously cared for being used by someone else and thrown in the dishwasher, or a guest feeling cold and grabbing one of his beloved Barbour jackets. In my email correspondence with this Marco guy, he confirmed he had actually moved back in and was renting the place out on weekends and that

he had every right to throw Jock's belongings out on the street, so I should be grateful that he hadn't done that yet. This was a father of young children, writing this to me in the weeks after we lost Jock. Extraordinary.

The kids had started at an international school in Rome, and had only been there for four days when Jock died and we raced back to Australia. We chose the school because the principal actually owned the school and the property it was on, and had started and grown the school herself. We liked that she was someone who cared so much, and who could make decisions, as the school was essentially her business. I emailed her to let her know what had happened, and asked – based on the fact the kids had only been there four days, the circumstances of them not returning, and the financial situation I was now in given all our income had come from Jock – if she would consider refunding some or all of the fees we had paid in advance for the remainder of the year. She responded once saying she would come back to me, and then never responded to my emails ever again.

Jock had many experiences in his life that created trauma scars and demons that he was never able to recover from. His exterior was that of a tattooed, sweary Scotsman; most would think that nothing could penetrate it and affect him. But the man I was gifted was beautifully broken; he so deeply wanted to love and be loved, and he went in and out of believing in his capability for those two things. In

the safety of the home and the family we created together, Jock was protected and loved unconditionally. One of the greatest robberies of Jock's death was that he was working towards healing his trauma; he wasn't just gliding through life anymore, thinking it would fix itself. He had never been healthier or fitter – he was eating salads, going on bushwalks, doing yoga – and he was educating himself on how to look some of his demons in the eye and move past them. He had admitted to himself that to have a happy family, he also needed to be happy. I wanted that for him as well; he deserved that. He was such a good man – imperfect, but a good human.

I think the people who had Jock and me in their lives, in partnership, whether that was personally or professionally, would say that we were symbiotic. We were two people with the majority of ourselves enmeshed in each other; we spent most of our waking hours together or communicating. For the first few years of *MasterChef*, I worked from the set, from his trailer and from the control room. He wanted me to be close, to support him as he stepped into this role, and also to take it all in so I could help guide him. He made me feel very valued and included. As Jock went into the *MasterChef* world, the amount of work escalated, and I took it all on with enthusiasm and confidence that we would get it done.

I came from a marketing, brand and business strategy background and those skills transferred seamlessly to

Jock's work. An opportunity would come to us from an advertising agency for one of their clients, and I would call them back and evolve the idea with them, then be part of the team that produced it. It meant everyone was winning – Jock was getting great jobs, the execution was fine-tuned, and the agency was able to talk and work with me in a language we both understood.

Alfie was 18 months old when Jock started on *Master-Chef*. Very soon after, I was pregnant with Isla, and then we had a newborn and a toddler in the house. I took a few days off with Isla, and then work kicked back off again. It kept escalating and escalating to the point where I didn't have time to eat. I would watch how much water I drank because I didn't have the time to go to the bathroom. I was at my desk by 5 am each day, crawling into bed hours after the kids had gone to sleep. On the days we were shooting content for Jock's socials, I was covered in sweat from sunrise till sunset as I was in charge of too much and was running around the office and set. I was looking after Jock's wardrobe, prepping the set for each shot, shortlisting crockery and cutlery so Jock could decide what each dish would be served on, helping to write recipes, taking behind-the-scenes footage for socials, making coffees and organising lunches for Jock and the crew, and handling countless other tasks. That, on repeat, is only sustainable for a period of time. I was also finding the work emotionally draining – managing

Jock was more than a one-person job, and it was increasingly difficult to be rational when I was doing his deals. I was also trying to keep him away from the chaos so he could have a clear mind each day as he went onto the set or as he walked into an interview. It was irrational to think I could do it all, but that only became obvious later. At the time, I just wanted to make sure Jock didn't have to carry too much, and before I knew it, the majority of the responsibility for our life and most of the work was falling on my shoulders.

Then one day, when I was crying at my desk because I didn't know how I could possibly do the work that needed to be done, Jock said he was going to head to the markets and asked what I felt like for dinner, and I lost my shit. I was working even harder as we had set our Rome plan in motion and I needed to get through an excessive amount of face-to-face work before we flew out. I closed my laptop and told him I was not working anymore. I wasn't even going to have a work conversation; he was going to have to figure it out. I think this was a breakdown. And it came only months before Jock's death, so I was already broken and unhealthy when I lost him. I went into traumatic loss and grief when I was already on my knees, making any recovery from this feel like an impossible task.

I walked into my relationship with Jock with my eyes wide open. I knew there was a chance that Jock could

break me with the weight of what he had lived through, and was constantly living through. But the way I have been broken is not what I expected and is in no way something he purposefully caused. Nevertheless, I am broken.

Forever Decisions

Grief, I discovered, was stacked full of decisions I couldn't undo or change. The biggest ones for me were deciding whether to bury or cremate Jock, and then where his resting place would be.

If Jock had a say, he would have told me to make the least amount of fuss. To cremate him and throw him into a loch in the Scottish Highlands and get on with things. But the thought of throwing him to the wind, him being gone forever, immediately felt wrong. I physically felt a firm 'no'. The kids and I were now homeless; our apartment in Rome had been abandoned, and we had no place to call home. That made the choice of a final resting place extra difficult, and it was a decision that needed to be made quickly. First I had to work out where to house the kids – Sydney was my home when I met Jock, and Ava lived there, so that

was where we headed. It then made sense that Jock was also there, and another forever decision was made.

The funeral planning was also urgent, but there were so many obstacles and decisions to make. I really had no idea how a funeral with so much public attention could be organised. I was speaking to Bev, the CEO at Network 10, most days, and during one conversation I admitted I was overwhelmed by not knowing how to arrange something that had so many moving parts and was so urgent, or how I could possibly keep it private. She said she would organise an event manager she trusted to work on it full-time with me and would also continue to provide us with security, as well as security advice on how to keep the day as private as possible. It was this team that shortlisted the chapels in Sydney and helped me to select a burial spot for Jock that would give us more seclusion on the day as well as into the future.

I am happy with the burial spot I chose for Jock. It's a double-decker spot next to bushland, so he is surrounded by beautiful eucalyptus trees and the constant sound of birds. It also means that I will be laid to rest with him there, which makes me happy. There was another spot I thought Jock would like because it was in the super old and creepy section, where the headstones were damaged, the stone angels had broken wings and it was all unkempt, a bit like a Halloween set-up. He would have loved it there, and he would have found it funny, but it wasn't private.

Now when we visit Jock, there is lots of grass and space for the kids: they sit with Jock and tell him stories, they sing him songs, they lie with their tummies down on the grass on top of Jock, propped up on their elbows, like they're lying on his chest having a chat. We take a picnic blanket out there for Father's Day and his birthday and we have a meal with him. It is exactly the spot he should be.

As I started making funeral decisions, I found that everyone wanted intel on what was happening so the story could be given to the media. This became a real problem when I needed to speak to suppliers: progress and speed were hampered because every supplier, whether I would use them or not, was asked to sign a non-disclosure agreement preventing them from speaking to the media. We also had to use fake names to throw people off the scent. It was a ridiculous added pressure at a time when I was already on the brink of breaking.

This period was also the beginning of my inability to move at any speed or with any intention; everything was now uphill in the dark. My usual intelligence completely disappeared. I became capable of one thought or action at a time; I had to really concentrate on listening when people were talking to me. There was no structure, order or habits, no familiarity that gave me guardrails to operate within. All I wanted was some peace, some silence in my mind and my environment, some stillness. It is that still-ness, which I still crave now, many months later, that I

don't think can ever return to my world. Grief cancels out stillness, and grief is now an extra limb that I can't live without. Grief strangely brings comfort to me; I feel a closeness to Jock that is just mine and is impossible to explain to the unbroken, those who live without trauma or unexpected catastrophic loss.

Every conversation anyone had with me for the first six months or so was hard – there was always a problem, something that would make me upset, something that I wouldn't like – and every call required a decision, which meant waiting for my mushy brain to answer in slow motion. The impairment of traumatic loss is real, and the first step in rebuilding for me was to be kind to myself and recognise that I could never be the person I was again. I will forever be a new person with the strange gift of being allowed a second chance to reinforce myself in the weak areas so that I become superhuman. All I hope is that as I rebuild, the reinforcements hold, because each stone placed takes so much effort and determination.

There have been difficult personal decisions too, many of which I know other widows have had to make. What to do with my wedding band and engagement ring was one of these. I was torn by the decision. I wore them, then I moved them onto my other hand, I moved them back again, I just wore the engagement ring, I put them on a necklace around my neck, I took them off. I'm still not sure what the permanent position will be; maybe I

will always use them as a comforting tool or as a measure of how I'm travelling. As I write this, I'm sitting in Italy, and I don't think I could handle having my rings on here. I would probably fiddle with them constantly and talk to Jock out loud as I did it. Or I'd look at them, and they would be a time machine, taking me back to the days we spent together in Italy, happy and truly living.

I also had to decide how to speak about Jock to the kids. They talk about him nonstop; they ask how much did Papa kiss me, and want to know if Papa got sad or made mistakes. One morning Alfie came into my bedroom and asked if I was lonely. I told him I missed Papa but I wasn't lonely. And he said that a man needed to sleep with me and then I wouldn't be lonely anymore. I asked him what he meant, and he said that children needed a mamma and papa, and so was I going to get another papa? I hadn't expected this observation – a mix of concern, confusion and comprehension – from my beautiful little boy, and I certainly hadn't thought about a response. But I wanted to answer in a way that gave him clarity, so I told him that Papa was my husband, that to me we were still married and I loved him more and more every day that passed. But the most important thing was that he was forever their papa; that was something that no one other than him could ever be. Alfie touched my cheeks with both his hands, cradling my face in his tiny little palms, gave me lots of kisses, then walked away. A moment in time for his inquisitive mind, days of sadness that followed for me.

A House of Mourning

Once I made the decision that Jock's final resting place would be in Sydney, the process of moving him from Melbourne to Sydney started. The funeral directors were going to fly him to Sydney, and in order to do so, he would have to be embalmed. My body physically reacted to that word; there was no way I was going to let that be done to Jock. Even now, I'm not entirely certain what embalming is or what it means, but my immediate reaction was a firm 'no'. I felt protective of him; I wanted him to finally find peace, without people touching him or looking at him. I just wanted him to be left alone.

This meant the only way to move Jock to Sydney was by road – he didn't need to be embalmed for that. I actually preferred this option for many reasons, but mainly because it meant I could stay with him as he was being moved.

I could be by his side, and feel that I was keeping him safe and protected. The drive to Sydney was going to take ten or so hours, so I asked my friend JT if he could drive me behind Jock. After some conversations that didn't involve me, he gently but strongly advised against it as they would need to change vehicles at the border into New South Wales, which would involve moving Jock between the two vehicles. I don't think he felt I could watch that happening, but also, more importantly, the media were looking for my face everywhere, so if someone did see me on that journey, they would literally have eyes on Jock, and it would be impossible to shake them after that.

I have always felt the need to protect Jock; it was part of my silent vow to him that I was his protector no matter what. And since he had died, the media could write anything they wanted about him with no repercussions. He was now defenceless and the depth of my protectiveness grew day by day. It was also making me extremely upset and anxious to see what was being written, and it felt like the stories would never stop. So we made a decision as a family that from that day forward any information about Jock wouldn't be for public consumption, and I committed to never reading an article about him again.

I didn't want Jock to be alone. I hated that thought. But I did eventually agree with the rationale for not driving behind him. I pulled together some things that we could

put with Jock for his journey – photos of him with each of the children, and one of us; Walker's shortbread, his worry beads, some Scotch whisky and, of course, Tunnock's Teacakes. Writing this now, it feels a bit childish for some reason, but it gave me comfort when agreeing that he could travel without me. Once all the items were together, Joey dropped them off at the Coroners Office, and they made sure they were placed in the vehicle with Jock.

We returned to Sydney and continued with the funeral planning. There were so many curve balls, so many security precautions and so many delicate decisions to be made. I also had to keep my location under wraps, or it would be back to The Prison and days of not being able to go outside.

Then it came time to work out what to bury Jock in. One of the hundreds of decisions I didn't know needed to be made, but the answers came naturally to me; I knew him as if he were me. It was, of course, one of his kilts – I just couldn't work out which one. He had had two kilt sets made in Scotland for his fortieth birthday, but I wanted those to be there for Alfie when he was older. I had spent a whole day in a dusty kilt shop while Jock got measured up and chose the exact stitching style and colour he wanted, the buttons for the jacket and the fit he was looking for on the shirt. They even customised one of the sporrans because it wasn't exactly what he wanted. Possibly one of the longest and most boring days of my life, but now a beautiful part of the kilt story for his only son. We had

finished that day having a fish and chips supper with a pot of tea, and all was forgiven.

When I couldn't work out the kilt question, I called Charz, one of Jock's closest friends who also put together his wardrobe at *MasterChef*, and asked her what I should do. She instantly agreed with my decision to keep all of Jock's favourites for Alfie. She still had all of Jock's kilts and accessories at *MasterChef*, so she said she would package me up an outfit with all the kilt pins and socks, the cufflinks, shirt and tie, everything she knew Jock would love.

The next thing to decide on was shoes. Jock only had one pair of ghillie brogues, and I wanted to keep them. I called Jane Barnes, wife of Jimmy and an absolute rock during this time, and asked if she knew where I could get another pair quickly. She said to send her a photo and his size and she would take care of it. She also said she had someone coming to do a kilt fitting for Alfie, so he would have a new one for the funeral. Jock and I had only bought Alfie one kilt his whole life – for his first Christmas, to match Jock's. Every other one of Alfie's kilts has been from Jane and Jimmy Barnes.

A few days later, we had just finished dinner at my friends' place, where the kids and I were staying, when the doorbell rang. My friends opened the door to Jane and Jimmy. The shoes and Alfie's kilt outfit were ready, and they had also found me a Lion Rampant flag to be draped

over Jock's coffin. They had dropped what they were doing and driven half an hour to bring them over late at night; Jane still had her apron on as she had been cooking all day and night for Jock's wake. They came in, loaded with cakes and biscuits that Jane had made for us, and headed for the kitchen, where my family were gathered, along with a few of my friends. Jimmy walked in chatting, and there was a shocked silence throughout the house. I had become used to awkward silences the last couple of weeks, so it didn't land on me that this was a different version. Jane and Jimmy were some of our closest friends, and at some point you just forget how famous Jimmy actually is. Jock and him were like brothers, and I think the kids saw that connection and also feel very close to Jimmy.

Jane and Jimmy stayed for a bit, then came into my bedroom and lay on my bed with me as I showed them the video I was going to play at the funeral; then they gave me enormous hugs and headed home. When I came out of my room, everyone was laughing and talking about how crazy it was that Jimmy Barnes was just in the kitchen. Like actually talking to them. It gave me a laugh, something that I was very much in need of.

The day before the funeral, I went to see Jock again. His outfit had been sent on ahead so that I could see him dressed in his kilt. It was going to be the last time I would see him. Joey and JT came with me, and I was directed through the building to where Jock was. It was a

calm room, with low lighting, candles burning, some bottles of water and a box of tissues. Jock was lying, fully dressed in his kilt, surrounded by the items I had pulled together for his trip from Melbourne to Sydney. I had left all of those things with him so he could be buried with them the next day. Seeing Jock brought me comfort; spending time with him was beyond difficult but it gave me extra moments with him that I would never get again. I touched his hair and his face again, and felt more confident in touching his body than I had at the Coroners Office. His hands were crossed over on his stomach, and I just wanted to hold them. I wanted him to touch my cheek one last time. But I didn't have the courage to take his hands in mine. I didn't know how I would feel holding the weight of them, and I was right on the edge of sanity after 11 days of being completely drained of everything I had, so I touched rather than held his hand. I could feel a difference in him: he wasn't there anymore. His spirit was somewhere else, more likely next to me than in his body.

I left the room, and JT asked if it would be okay if he went in to say goodbye. I said of course. Jock still had his wedding band on, and I wanted to keep it for the kids, so I asked JT if he could request someone to remove it for me. He told me it would be his honour to remove it for me himself. When he came out from seeing Jock, he put it in my hand, and I held it the whole way home. Before bed that night, I put it on my necklace so I could keep it

on me. Joey asked if she could go in and see Jock after JT. She noticed that Jock's worry beads were in his hand and not wrapped around his knuckles and palm like they usually would be, so she lifted his hand and placed them correctly. These actions of JT's and Joey's seem so small, but they were huge gestures of care and maturity that I am not sure I could have performed if the positions had been reversed.

By the time we left it was dark outside, but no one was rushing me to be finished. It was the last night before the unknown of Jock's funeral, and it was all I could think about as I was driven home. I wanted so much to have privacy, but I knew that wouldn't happen; it was really going to be a matter of how much our privacy would be destroyed.

In the early hours of the next morning, Alfie crept into my bed. He saw Jock's wedding band on my necklace for the first time, and he kissed it, cuddled me, then went back to his bed. Jock was happy I had it.

The Funeral

On the day of the funeral, it dawned on me that my new role as a widow was about to begin. Other than seeing Jock and travelling to Sydney, I hadn't been outside in two weeks, and the media wanted to get a shot of me out and about, preferably crying. I had agreed with Network 10, Jock's employer, on certain things; one was that they could have a camera outside at the funeral. Let me be really clear – they put absolutely no pressure on me at any point. I didn't need to agree to anything to get their support; I didn't need to say 'yes' to them airing Jock's last season of *MasterChef*. They were navigating this situation for the first time, personally and with kindness, and I was so grateful to have the support of a team that cared for Jock and wanted the best for his children and for me. I was advised, not by Network 10,

that if we gave the media some information and promised them some footage, then they would be less desperate to seek it out themselves, which we knew they would do at any cost. So we gave them a few quotes from my eulogy and from Ava's. I mention this because I saw afterwards that some people were upset that the cameras were there and thought guests had leaked the quotes. What is true is that one of the guests told the media the location and time of the funeral. I am 99 per cent certain who this was: she works in the media and told a colleague. But the quotes from inside the chapel came from me agreeing to provide them, not someone doing the wrong thing.

Andy and Alex had been trapped in their house, or followed when they left it, for two weeks now and had been spotted at Sydney airport, when they arrived a couple of days before the funeral. It was important to Ava and me that they be included in the family stuff that was happening before and after the funeral, and we both wanted them to be able to come to my friends' place, where the kids and I were staying, to join the procession to the funeral. Network 10 was looking after their movements, and security was made aware of our request and started working on how they could transport Andy and Alex to join us. Andy was a pallbearer, but even if he wasn't, I would have wanted them to be with us and to move to and from the funeral in privacy, with each other there for comfort. Every option was considered, then decoy cars

were deployed to ensure their privacy. That meant Andy and Alex had to sit in a car for an extra four or so hours to see if they were being followed and to make sure they were well clear of their hotel before any media started waiting out the front. Another unfair burden on two people who had lost a dear friend and were already in the throes of anxiety and devastation on the day of his funeral.

We had five cars carrying Ava and me, my family and our best friends. Three cars waited in the back laneway, the other two out the front. I went out to my assigned car in the laneway, where I met my dad. This was the first time I had seen him, and he gave me a defeated hug, summing up that he never thought he would be at his daughter's husband's funeral. He gave me one of his handkerchiefs, the first of a few I swiped from him that day. Also standing there patiently, like an enormous statue, was Cargs – a man, a friend, who knew Jock and me better than we knew ourselves. He embraced me, and reassured me of what I already knew – I had him as my friend forever. A few streets away, Andy and Alex's car was driving aimlessly, waiting to join the procession as we all went to say goodbye to a man we loved.

Ava sat next to me as we drove into a storm I didn't think either of us could weather. I could write a whole book on Ava – the beautiful girl I first met, the woman she has become, the support she has been to me in every moment of my grief and joy. She is the female version

93

of Jock and I feel such safety in knowing she is part of my life. She is fierce like him, she has an enormous heart like him and she will live an even fuller and more meaningful life because she lost him. Since Jock's death, Ava has sensed when I need to be propped up, when I need to be told I'm a good mum, a good friend, that it will all be okay. She is the one person I believe when they say those things, and I have her with me forever. She is a part of Jock and she knows the man he was and the man he wanted to be; we share that knowledge and care for him, and that makes our bond what it is.

The service started at 11 am, and we arrived 15 minutes before that. Security called our driver to advise that everyone was seated inside the chapel, and in the background of the call I heard the bagpipes playing, as did Ava. Dougie, a close friend of Jane and Jimmy's who Jock had met plenty of times, was giving Jock a heartfelt Highland send-off. Ava and I were already holding hands, and now we squeezed each other without any care for how hard, or any apology. A sickening tsunami of reality swept over me – this was real, and it was all about to start. I really appreciated that all of our friends had shown respect by getting there early; had connected and cared for each other, and then moved into their seats so we could arrive and get started when we were ready.

The convoy did a U-turn, and we made our way through the gates to the chapel, a road I have taken hundreds of

times since. Driving into a cemetery is sombre; this gave me a feeling of sickness that I couldn't shift for hours. We drove slowly up to the chapel, our car at the front, and I saw Jock's coffin in the hearse for the first time. It was draped in the Lion Rampant flag, with beautiful lily, thistle and heather flowers covering it. The arrangements had been made by a florist in Sydney who Jock had bought flowers from for me over the years.

I stayed in the car while everyone else got out and walked into the chapel and to their seats at the front. Andy walked Alex inside to her seat; I didn't know if she was going to be able to get through the service and worried it would be too much for her. Losing Jock really hit her – it still affects her profoundly now when we speak about him – and with Andy acting as a pallbearer she would have to get through the initial moments by herself.

They moved Jock's coffin out of the hearse, and Uncle Terry performed a smoking ceremony. I imagined Jock stretched out peacefully, his eyes closed, breathing in the smoke in long, deep breaths as he did at all smoking ceremonies. When Uncle Terry finished, I realised how quiet it was. There was no music, just silence. And Jock resting, waiting for us to carry him inside the chapel.

I sat in the car for as long as I could, and then it was time for me to step into being a widow, to show my face, and hope I could handle what was in front of me. I got out of the car, the smell of bushfire in the air. My brother, Joel,

was there waiting for me, and he put his hand protectively around my back. Andy had returned to help carry Jock, and we hugged. We hadn't seen each other in over a week and we were both looking at the ground; we didn't want to make eye contact.

Looking back at that moment of stepping out of the car, I see how disempowering it was. I wanted to show strength, to carry my gorgeous husband with love and pride and absolute capability into his funeral. I had him, I always had him. I could protect him and help him find peace. But it felt like I couldn't genuinely be me because there were so many cameras only metres away. I felt unfairly exposed.

As I walked into the chapel, one hand on Jock, I didn't see many faces. I saw Pauly, Jock's mate from Kangaroo Island, who he dived for scallops with, and Dave, his mate from his early Adelaide days. Both were distraught, absolutely broken, and I touched them, hoping they understood I was trying to say we'll all be okay. We got Jock to the front of the room and I sat down next to Ava. We hugged. My sister, Lani, was sitting directly behind us, close by to support me. She had one hand on my shoulder most of the service, and I needed that. Lani had stepped into her big sister role with all the care and love it is possible to show, both for me and my children. We've had all of the usual sister stuff over the years, but she is my person. We have lived our lives concurrently; she understands and accepts all the versions of me, and I have really needed her since

the moment I found out I had lost Jock. The kids gravitate to her, which says everything to me. I love her beyond words, and they are words I don't say enough. But I will commit to that from here on.

Gregory, a dear friend of Jock's, was running the service for us, and he had already said a few words prior to our arrival, reminding everyone that we were all sitting in our immense grief together and to respect the privilege of being in the same room for this moment. He also delicately explained that the day's emotional architecture would escalate and asked everyone to support each other through it.

Cargs spoke first, then Joey read an excerpt from Jock's book, *Last Shot*, and then it was Ava's time. She had asked Andy to stand with her, to take over if she couldn't finish. He was her willing protector and supporter, and I know Jock would have been so happy that she chose him to be her person that day. Unsurprisingly, Ava didn't need Andy to finish her eulogy; she was strong, courageous, and every word she spoke was perfect and real. They were hard words for her to get out; she had lost so much when she lost Jock. The majority of the people in the room had watched her grow up and now witnessed her courage and strength as a woman. She showed them the depths of her grief and that she was grateful for Jock, for being his daughter. They all held her through the 20 minutes or so of her eulogy, as she articulated her love and loss, the friendship she and her dad

had created through choice not obligation, and then she took a breath and came to sit back down. This cemented her shift from Jock's child to Jock's adult daughter.

I had chosen Jock's carbonara recipe as one of the readings. It was one of his favourite things, but I also needed a breather between Ava's eulogy and my own. Lani had been going to read it, but the day before, Jake, her nine-year-old son, asked if he could do it. When Lani asked me, I was so proud of him. Jake was the first child in my life who I can say I truly loved; he was born, and I just wanted him to be mine. Years later, we had Alfie, and he is a little version of Jake, which I love. Seeing Jake standing up the front next to Jock's coffin, delivering the carbonara recipe, made me feel immensely proud again; he was so brave and suddenly so grown up, doing his mumma's reading in a room full of strangers. Jock always had a special place in his heart for Jake; he would have loved that Jake was stepping into this responsibility and doing this for him. I could imagine Jock shaking his hand afterwards and saying, 'Bloody brilliant, mate, you nailed it!'

But now it was my time. I took my notes and the last pair of worry beads that Jock had used, which I had found in his jeans pocket, and walked up to the podium. To be standing next to my love saying his eulogy didn't feel right. As I started speaking, I didn't care how I sounded, or that anyone was even in the room; I was saying words that I wanted Jock to hear. I wanted my impossibly gorgeous

husband to hear my words and leave this world knowing them. I felt cheated, I felt abandoned, I felt like I had been left behind to work it all out on my own. I found myself thinking that these were the last words I would be able to say to Jock, and as I told myself that, I felt like I was losing control. My body was hot then cold; I lost all moisture in my mouth, and then my nose wouldn't stop running. It really was my body mirroring my emotions, which were absolute chaos.

I found writing Jock's eulogy a simple, albeit heart-breaking, task. I wrote what I felt, which meant it didn't have the structure of a regular eulogy where you say the person's date and location of birth, and then all their life milestones from there. Eulogies are meant to be a celebration of someone's life, with a few basic jokes sprinkled in to give comic relief from the intensity of it all, but I was too immensely devastated to be able to do that for the people in the room. I wrote of the life we had together, with his children, and what he meant to us. I read it again now and I see how hopeless everything felt when I wrote it – it all felt unfair and confusing, and I was in so much pain. I also see now that I wrote it in the present tense as if he were still alive, something I didn't realise at the time.

I wrote Jock so many love letters and long birthday and Christmas cards during our life together – I always found it so natural to explain my love and admiration for him, and I think when you adore someone like I adored

him it is easy. In retrospect, I can say I am proud of myself for delivering the eulogy, and I know Jock would have been proud of me. I'm normally hysterical at funerals, but somehow I managed to keep it mostly together. Everything felt surreal. I kept asking myself how I was even there and what was actually happening. As I finished my eulogy, I felt no relief; just a heaviness that I didn't think life could move on from. It was like I was looking at this enormous void, and trying to adjust to it now being what life looked and felt like. I sat back down and leant into Ava's arms. I held her hands and wished to be transported out of there.

The pain of it all was debilitating; I felt like I was wandering around in a fucking nightmare. Then the nightmare intensified. It was time for Jock to leave, for us to say goodbye to him and lay him to rest. I gave Jock's worry beads, still gripped tight in my hand, to Lani, and then the five boys and I lifted him onto our shoulders. With my head bowed in an attempt to create some privacy, I held on to the handle like I was holding Jock's hand before jumping off a cliff – firmly and trusting that I was going to be alright. With Dougie playing the bagpipes as our soundtrack, we carried Jock out to the hearse.

Griefnesia

I hadn't brought Alfie and Isla to the chapel for the service as there was no way of getting them in and out without being photographed by the media. I didn't want the kids to see images of themselves on that day later in life, and I didn't want them to have any memory of experiencing such unnecessary exposure. It was up to me to keep them safe, and the best way to do that was to keep them away from the service.

The family and friends from the car convoy who were still inside the chapel were taken out a side door, and the pallbearers got into cars and an enormous blacked-out bus and headed in different directions. I sat back in my car by myself, following behind Jock, in silence but not stillness, and didn't know where I was going or what I was doing. Just sitting and letting the current take me. JT saw me in

the car alone, ran over and opened the door, and sat in the back seat with me. He held my hand, and I squeezed it tightly. I remember releasing him minutes later and us just looking at each other. He said he didn't want me to be alone, and he was right. As we were driving away from the chapel, there were people standing there taking photos and videos of Jock's coffin. Not the media, just everyday people who wanted to capture that moment. I still don't understand that.

Our strategy as we left the chapel was to make the media assume that Jock was being cremated, so the cars drove us to the crematorium, and we walked through there to another chapel, where we reconvened outside. We had whisky and Tunnock's Caramel Logs while the crowd dispersed, and we all caught our breath, then it was time to bury my gorgeous husband. Alfie and Isla had arrived by now, Alfie in his little kilt that Jimmy and Jane had given him, wee Isla in a navy, nearly black, dress, her sad eyes wondering what all of this was about. They were clinging onto my legs; everything in them said this was not a good day.

I had explained to the kids what we were doing. I had told them that Papa was going to be buried in the ground, and they would put dirt and grass on top of him. And then we could come back and visit any time we wanted. My therapist, Tanya, had counselled me through the decisions for this day, and she felt that it was important the

kids understood the ritual of burial if it was a place I was going to bring them back to. At the time I agreed in theory, and now I know that was absolutely the right decision for them both.

When we arrived at the burial spot, Alfie got out of the car with me and saw Jock's coffin in the hearse. He seemed a bit angry and said I had told him Papa was in a box, and this was not a box. As I reflect on this time, the only thing that I regret is not explaining to the kids what a coffin is and that Papa would be inside one. In Alfie's mind, a box was made out of cardboard, so when he saw the coffin he got upset and said that Papa wouldn't be able to get out of that. It wasn't the image he had in his mind; this was all much more permanent and confusing. Cargs was there listening to the conversation, and now he took Alfie's hand and asked the man to bring Jock out of the hearse so Alfie could be closer and not looking at him through the window. This helped Alfie; I also think that being heard by an adult and given time to process things was what he needed.

Everyone was now standing around the burial spot, and the pallbearers and I went to lift Jock again. Alfie said, 'I'm helping.' I told him the coffin was really heavy and we had no handles left, so he could hold my hand and help me carry Papa. Our brave little boy walked hand in hand with me as we carried Jock to his final resting place. Forever best friends. As we placed Jock

in position, Alfie ran over to Bronwyn, JT's wife and one of my best friends, for a cuddle. Then I stepped back. I had Ava on one side and Isla on the other. Now I could let go; I didn't have to be anything or hide anything, I could just let the grief overwhelm me.

From this point through to the wake at Jimmy and Jane's house, I have only fragmented memories of what happened. It was my first experience of griefnesia, something that has constantly destroyed my mind and memory since. My recall of the rest of the burial is incomplete; I looked out, but it was all a blur. I did see one of my best friends, Nat, during the service. She is always a beacon of positivity and understanding, so it made sense that my eyes would rest on her for comfort. I also saw Sabrina, our doctor, who had saved Alfie's life – someone who had been with Jock and me through some of our toughest moments.

Bronwyn is an opera singer, and she sang the 'Celtic Blessing'. Then Gregory said a few words before Jimmy and Mahalia, his daughter, sang 'Caledonia' – Jock's favourite song, which he'd sung to the kids every night when they were in bed – with Ben, Jimmy's son-in-law, on the guitar. At the wake, I was surprised when people spoke about how beautifully Jimmy and Mahalia had sung together at the burial. I could have sworn on my life that they hadn't sung – I had no memory of it. My body and mind had shut down; it was like the emergency switch had been flicked and I was gifted complete darkness.

Much of what happened I have pieced together from talking with my family and friends, but I do remember that as Jock was being lowered into the earth, a gust of wind came up, and the Lion Rampant flag began to fly off the coffin – it looked like it was going into the grave. I screamed out, 'No!' and JT jumped forward, stopping it from going in and putting it back in position. Alfie started crying loudly and ran towards the coffin, trying to stop Jock from being lowered; he wanted to get in there with him. It was such a gesture of innocence, his reaction to his papa being taken away from him. I grabbed him, and held him tightly on my lap, kneeling on the grass next to Jock. Alfie wanted to be close to Jock, so we sat as near to the edge as we could. I told Alfie that Papa was going to be alright and that we had to let him go – we had no choice – and we leant over and watched Jock disappear from our world.

Alfie started screaming questions – 'Can Papa even breathe in there? Is he cold? Did you give him one of the Scottish blankets? Did you give him a pillow, Mamma? What if he needs to go to the toilet?' Then, after the dirt had been filled to the top, he asked where Papa's grass was, we needed that now. I told the kids we could stay for as long as we needed; there was no rush to be anywhere. That's when Alfie said, 'Papa, sit up and get out of the box!' He has said that to Jock a few times when we have visited him since. He screams it so loudly I'm not sure if he thinks Jock won't hear him or he's letting his anger out.

As the service finished, Gregory told everyone that they could stay or go, whatever felt right for them, but to let us have some time alone as a family. By now, Alfie and Isla weren't crying, they were screaming through tears. It was an expression of grief that I never want to hear again, one where they lost their breath, where they cried and no words came out. Alfie's voice went hoarse as noises that were not words or even cries came from him. I don't know how long I sat on the grass next to Jock, our son on my lap slowly calming down, Ava on the grass next to us. But everyone was facing away when I eventually got up and walked our three children away from their dad towards the car. I don't think they could handle watching this moment unfold, the unjustness of it, the robbery that our little family was trying to come to terms with. I wished I could turn away from it too, but the kids needed the opposite of that.

I remember seeing the kookaburras as we left the cemetery, but then the griefnesia overwhelmed me again. I don't remember how we got to the wake. No part of me had wanted to have one. I understand their benefits, that they help everyone close out the day, but I couldn't talk to people. Jimmy and Jane were my guardian angels. They invited us to return to their home and have a small and private meal, which I was immensely grateful for. Their family and best friends had spent the day setting tables, making food and getting everything prepared,

but then disappeared when we arrived, only to return later to help clean it all up – one of the greatest gifts we could have received from the Barnes family and their friends.

Hiding Away

I had hoped that after the funeral the media attention would fade away. But every day, the articles kept coming, with no fresh news in them because there was really nothing new to tell. I had gone into a media blackout for the weeks after Jock's death and stayed away from social media. There were two times when people in the media notified me of stories that were being worked on that were so staggering to them they wanted me to know. I was then able to protect Jock and ensure the truth was told or that the story didn't happen. Of the very limited number of articles I have read since, not one of them is factual. There is no way I could combat them all; the reporting was like a runaway train of misinformation that kept being syndicated and quoted as fact all around the world. I had to focus any energy I had left on the important tasks, not on the media.

Even though I wanted to find a new house, settle the kids down and get going on running away from this grief, I couldn't be in Sydney and have any privacy. We hid away at my sister's place up the coast – Manno, my brother-in-law, made the kids pancakes and me gin and tonics, Jakey read books and played the guitar for his cousins, and Lani sat with me hour after hour just listening, and looked after the kids so I could go for walks on the beach by myself.

Then we went to JT and Bronwyn's beach shack in the bush a few hours south of Sydney, where they helped me with the kids 24/7. I have been friends with JT for maybe 15 years, and as we became close I also became close to Bron. Jock loved hanging out with them; he felt a rapport with both of them but I think he also could see their importance in my life, and how their maturity and life experience guided me. This was one of my friendships that he took over and made his own, and now at this time they were the ones I trusted and needed.

On the first day I was there, I rugged up and went for a long walk through the wind along the beach. And that's when I saw Jock. A guy in a Barbour jacket and Persol sunnies was sitting there with his dog. I walked towards him, closer and closer. I would have only been a few metres away, and it was 100 per cent him. I stopped. Then I walked away, feeling sick and telling myself I had to find a way to accept that Jock had actually died.

My therapist tells me this is normal and to be expected; my will for Jock to reappear and for this all to be a bad dream means I see him like this.

Ava came and joined us for the first week at the beach shack, and it was exactly what we needed. The kids and me together, with our most trusted friends, sitting in front of the fireplace, playing cards, cooking meals together. Jock and I had spent time with JT and Bron here before, and we had such a fun visit. In his usual larrikin way, the last time we were there, Jock had asked what the contraption was hanging from the wall in the kitchen. JT explained it was an antique meat rotisserie. That obviously got all of Jock's attention. JT explained how once it was wound up it clicked into a new position every hour to rotate the meat, and that it made a seriously loud and annoying sound when it did. So what did Jock do? He wound it up and it dinged every hour for a whole day and night, bouncing JT and Bron out of their sleep every hour that night. We all had a laugh about it the next day, some more than others (we were downstairs with Alfie so we didn't hear it ding all night). Then one night, when the kids and I were there, and we were playing cards, it dinged. No one had touched it, and no winding had occurred; I have no doubt that Jock willed it to happen so we would feel his presence. That antique meat rotisserie thing had been on that wall for decades and never dinged without being wound up, but that night it did.

That week at the beach shack, I finished reading a book written by a guy who specialises in grief, specifically traumatic grief experienced after mass shootings or by those who work on the frontline. He had unexpectedly lost his 21-year-old son. He spoke of the process he went through and said that for at least the first year, he found that he didn't laugh; he didn't even smile. That made me extremely sad, and it was another blow to any hope I had of us being okay. That night, Ava and I were in our usual position in front of the fireplace playing cards with JT, Bron and their adult daughter Phoebe, having a couple of wines and chatting. And before I even realised it was happening, Ava and I were laughing. We weren't just giggling; we were laughing so hard that I thought I might wet my pants. My face was hurting, and I had to push my smile down at the sides because I couldn't handle the pain anymore. When I got into bed that night, I thought we had achieved a little victory. Together, Ava and I could keep living and enjoying life. But the big lesson for me was that the author's journey was not mine. He was not me; I had young children who needed energy in their day, and their happiness would be driven by mine. The same applies to anyone reading this now – I don't want to hide any parts of it or only write about the bits that give you hope. Grief is grief, but no two people's experiences of it are the same.

I hit the one-month mark when we were there, hidden away in the beach shack in the middle of beautiful

eucalyptus trees, which Jock adored. It was the day that JT and Bron headed back to Sydney, and I stayed on, just the little ones and me. That night, after they had left, I recorded my first video for Jock's Instagram to say thanks to everyone for their care and messages and ask what they thought I should do with his social channel. I knew Jock was loved but the response I received was nothing short of overwhelming. The shock and loss that people all over the world were feeling and trying hard to grapple with was beyond what I had expected. I also realised I had become someone that other people who had experienced loss wanted to connect with. I had no capacity for that; I had no skills or understanding of where to from here – it still felt like I was in the first few days of losing Jock.

As I read some of those messages I felt dread, and the tiny progress I had made reset to zero. It also made me angry that some of these people felt their grief was the same as mine. People were telling me that they had lost their husbands unexpectedly 15 years before and that they still couldn't get past it. Others told me that they had remarried but would never truly love again. Others spoke of the irreparable impact on their young children – one little boy had stopped talking and never started again. I knew sharing experiences was part of this new club I was in, and that being realistic about what the future looks like is actually an intelligent approach, but I couldn't bear to hear these stories. I felt like I wouldn't stand still; that the

side street I'd be taken down would be even worse than the road I was already on, and more and more problems would start to appear for me and for our children. Every day I would receive thousands and thousands of messages, and I had no idea what to do with them. I didn't want to ignore people in pain, but I couldn't absorb theirs either because it caused me so much fear about our future. The path from here sounded treacherous and miserable, and I wanted to block that out; otherwise, I felt, I would never emerge from the heavy cloud that was constantly surrounding me.

I found gratitude for many things very early on. One of them was that I have photos of Jock with the kids on pretty much every day of their lives. There's some of me here and there, but I was always capturing the moments, watching Jock with his little ones and wanting to savour that. Now, I have those moments, and they are what the children crave to see. They ask for specific photos – Isla will say, 'Can you show me a photo of Papa cooking with me?' Alfie will ask, 'Can you show me a photo of me eating gelato with Papa?' – and I have all of them. Isla asked me only recently to see a photo of the first time Papa cuddled and kissed her. Of course I had several and showed her, but it breaks my heart a little bit each time. The kids and I are all on different cycles of melancholy and sadness. Some days I don't want to show them photos or videos of Jock because I'm on the edge; at other times, they are. Only last night, Alfie asked me to sing him 'Caledonia',

which I do every night, and Isla said that she didn't want that song tonight because she was feeling a bit sad and that would make her more sad. So we all adapt to what the others want, and we prioritise someone's sadness and slowing down the momentum of sadness over our need for comfort.

Grief made me selfish – I lost touch with using my manners or asking how anyone else was; I didn't reply to calls or messages, and most of the time, I didn't even listen when people were talking to me. I was in a deep, dark well of pain, and no one could ever possibly understand it. I started reading another book about grief, written by a 30-year-old who had lost her mum to cancer. My grief lens at the time told me that the author was a grown woman who had been able to live her childhood and many of her adult years guided and loved by her mum. Then she found out she was going to lose her and was given nine months to say goodbye and prepare herself for the loss. I lost my shit – that's not grief, I thought, that's just life and it happens every day. But now, outside of that dark well of immediate loss, I feel nothing but care and sympathy for her; I imagine she is Ava. I think of the moments in Ava's life when she will want her dad to be there for her, and he won't be. I cry thinking about her not having Jock to walk her down the aisle, or having her first baby and not being able to share that moment with her dad. My grief lens was inward-facing and very much 'poor me', and I wish I hadn't

felt like that. If you are in that stage, be kind to yourself and know it's normal, and it will pass when you're ready.

A couple of months in I realised that I was no longer taking photos of the kids. I had stopped wanting to capture life, to bottle it up as something I could look at later. The only new photos I had were from my sister and my friends: some of me and the kids, others of the kids just being. I look at them now and see the date, and I'm grateful we have them. It captures a moment in our healing that I am really proud of, one that shows me that we were in it together and that every day we made progress. At the time, it felt like nothing was shifting and each day was just a repeat of the previous one. But in tiny increments, we were moving away from the impact zone and into our new world. It wasn't easy or fun, but the small shifts were adding up.

No Apologies

I stopped saying I was sorry. It was a word I realised I had used often before, and now didn't feel any need for in my vocab. If it wasn't life or death, it just didn't matter to me. This was the intense but very clear filter I used to survive and get through normal life, which can be challenging on a daily basis when you have little children. By not caring about anyone but the kids, I closed the circle of potential interference and had some level of control in my life again.

This also meant that I lost sight of what had meaning or was important to others. My simplified perspective on life was adopted without any malice or nastiness, and accepted by everyone. Concern and care were only going one way, and that was in my direction. If I was late for something, I didn't care. I stopped returning calls. Texts were like grains of sand, and I treated them as such. The number of

calls and texts, emails and messages through social media platforms I was receiving was extraordinary. There was no way to filter out what was critical, or what I would want to read, so I ignored them all.

I also lost any interest in seeing myself. I didn't look in the mirror when I was brushing my teeth or my hair. I didn't get dressed and quickly look in the mirror to make sure my outfit was in the right place and looked okay. It wasn't even about not caring how I looked – I just didn't want to see myself. I didn't want to catch my own eye and see that I had changed; I didn't want to witness what my face felt like. I knew how I felt, and that was miserable; seeing it would actually be believing it.

I adopted a mourning outfit by accident. Nearly all my clothes were still in Rome or in a shipping container on the way to Rome, so it felt almost acceptable that I wore the same outfit every day. It made life easier and meant I wasn't in my pyjamas all day; I was warm and comfortable, and no decisions needed to be made. I had made a lifetime of decisions and had nothing left to give. My mourning outfit was a pair of jeans I had bought in Rome, a black long-sleeve top I had a few of and my Scotoni tartan jacket with shearling on the inside. The jacket was from our favourite restaurant in the Dolomites in Italy, and wasn't something you could buy – our friends who owned Rifugio Scotoni had given it to me that year. It made me feel closer to Jock: we loved wearing our

matching Scotoni merch around, and skiing together in the Dolomites was our favourite holiday.

I had gone from washing and blowdrying my hair daily to doing almost nothing. A bit of dry shampoo and a bun was all I needed; most days I went to bed like that and woke up the next morning without redoing it. The kids used to run their fingers through my hair when I was cuddling them – Isla would twirl my hair between her fingers – and I only realise now that I took that connection point away from them at a time when they needed it more than ever.

Then, one day, six weeks in, I washed and blowdried my hair. I put on a different outfit, and I went for a walk. And that was the step forward I needed. It was also when I was brave enough to leave the house without tissues. I know that sounds like a small thing but it is a vivid milestone of progress for me. No one pushed me to that point, or said 'Let's take you out', or 'A walk would do you some good'. I got there naturally and was ready to go back to a part of what life used to be. What I found on this first walk was that I didn't want to be alone in my head, but I also didn't want to be with someone or talk to anyone I bumped into. I started listening to music all the time, building a new playlist of sad songs that evolved to include a greater range over time. I always had music playing, whether it was on in the house or on my headphones; I needed the constant sound of something. I dedicated my

walks to learning, to grief literature that would educate me on trauma, grief, loss, the physical impact of trauma, finding meaning, bringing up resilient children, restoring calm and habits, and the stories of people who had lived through and survived their version of this. My therapist, Tanya, also recommended books: some were easy reading and others were used to train therapists and went much deeper.

In the process of educating myself I was reaching out for my exact situation, and I couldn't find it. I would hear of people who lost their mum, their children, or whose partners were lost to terminal diseases. I needed my version mirrored: a big love, a couple meant to live their days together, with precious little children, living a life less ordinary and completely in tune with each other, all gone in one moment with no warning. Where was the playbook on how to survive that? Why was no one else's loss as deep or expansive as mine? Maybe I just wouldn't survive this.

My body felt depleted. I never found myself reaching for a glass of water; it was either coffee, wine or whisky. Every time I stood up I was dizzy. My skin was dehydrated, I always had headaches, my hair was breaking, my nails stopped growing. I was having full imaginary conversations with my dead husband. I had no ability to parent with patience or love. Why was no one talking about this in their podcasts or books? I needed to hear from someone in the thick of it; to share the experience

of one minute having clarity, then the next feeling like I was in the middle of a washing machine trying to thread a needle. It was impossible to think there was another side of this sick feeling, this constant confusion about what was happening and why.

Then, layer by layer, I reintroduced parts of my old life. I went out for lunch with two of my friends; I accepted an invitation for the kids to go to a friend's birthday party, and I said yes to friends flying from interstate to spend a few days visiting. And each time I said 'yes' it was the right decision. Then one day I told myself that I would just say 'yes' – if any of my friends or family asked me to do something, it was a 'yes' from me. If I felt like going out for a meal at Fratelli Paradiso, I would go. I figured that if I acted like everything was normal, one day it might be. And this was one of the secrets to my recovery. My year of 'yes' put me in the hands of friends who were trying to work out how to help me, and being with me and having fun together was something they could gift me. I have since extended it into a second year because the first one was so effective and memorable.

As I started going 'back to normal' I told myself to do certain things. One of the first tasks was to buy thankyou cards for everyone who had helped me in the months before. It was a challenge for me because I wanted them to be really nice; I felt they were a reflection of Jock. But my brain was so foggy that even searching for some online

tired me out and I couldn't make any decisions. After many hours of scrolling, I decided to pause on finding the perfect card, and start drafting what I would write to each person. Complete writer's block. In the past I had prided myself on writing cards with meaning to people. Now, I had nothing to say. I refused to be generic or repeat the message across cards. I figured that it would come to me eventually, so I went back to the card scrolling. I found the perfect cards, ordered them, and still now, not one has been despatched. It is one of the many things that the old version of me did but the current version of me won't let me do. It seems simple, possibly even irrelevant, but I think parts of my mind and heart have been so damaged they just don't light up anymore.

Five months in, the shipping container with our whole life packed inside arrived from Italy. It was only halfway there when Jock died, so it was a long wait for it to rebound back to us. And to be honest, I don't think I could have handled it any earlier. Jock had managed the house being packed up so the kids didn't have to see our life in boxes. The beauty of this arrangement was that Jock had decided what we would take into our new life in Rome. We had gone through each room and chatted about it, but he was the doer. It was like the universe gifted me the belongings that Jock loved, and now all the decisions have been made, I will keep those things forever. As I unpacked each item and decided whether I could fit it into our tiny

new home, I unwrapped a mix of memories and emotions. I would go from laughing that he had packed his sausage maker and scuba diving gear together in one box to seeing the leather cufflink box with 'JZ' embossed on it that I'd had made for him and having to walk away for a moment by myself to have a cry.

Unpacking our old life and incorporating it into our new one, seeing all of our artwork on the walls and Jock's most treasured possessions back with us, was so emotional it was nearly unbearable. I didn't realise we had accumulated so many meaningful family heirlooms, but having these parts of Jock around me, and knowing the kids could have them in their lives forever, did give me comfort. Jock's Scottish chair, the one I am sitting in now as I write this, has given me many hours of comfort, almost as if I am sitting next to him. It feels a bit stupid to even be writing this – it's just a chair, but he fell in love with it in the Scottish Highlands one year. After much effort and money, as well as a forklift and crate delivery, I surprised him with it on his birthday. It was in front of our fireplace and he sat there often, so it always seemed to be where we would gravitate when it was time to open birthday or Christmas presents. Many whiskies were enjoyed on this chair. And now it sits at the head of our dining table, and I eat all my meals at home from it. Jock and I referred to it as 'the Scottish chair' and now the kids refer to it as 'Papa's chair'. Sometimes I come into the room and find

them both wedged into it and they look up and say, 'We're being really careful.'

With the arrival of all of Jock's belongings, I entered a state of panic that things would get damaged and simply disappear from the world. Someone would be over and say they were going to make themselves a cup of tea and I would leap out of my chair to make sure they didn't use Jock's Tunnock's mug. Jock and I used the same wine glasses for any wine or champagne we would drink, and he had only packed two of these. They're in my cupboard now and if someone goes to get a wine glass, I pounce to make sure they don't choose Jock's one. And then there was the time Mum used the last of the sugar in the container next to the coffee machine and I was devastated because that was the last of the sugar that Jock had put in the container. I had also been using Jock's water bottle that he had on him when he died and it took me months and months to make the decision to put it in the dishwasher. I didn't want to wash away any trace of him. Absurd, I recognise that now. But at the time I wanted our world and every item inside it to be protected and wrapped in cotton wool. My fear of irreplaceable things being broken embedded fear in the kids, and I hated myself for that. They would want to touch Jock's belongings, but didn't because they thought I might get upset. They understand now that some things can't be replaced if they're broken, but that Papa would have let them touch anything, so if they do, they just need

to do their best to be careful. If something breaks, we clean it up, and I'm allowed to be sad, but I'm not allowed to be angry.

With our old life now merged into our new one, my mind decided that none of this was real, and I would sit out the front of the house for hours during the course of the day, waiting to see Jock's head pop up above our fenceline. A fenceline that he had never walked past before, belonging to our home he had never even entered.

Things to Say

Losing Jock was so public, so international, that there was no one who knew Jock or me who didn't know my husband had died. And then there were all the people who didn't know Jock personally but could relate to him and felt a connection to him. In their helplessness and loss they reached out to me to show their support. Jock really enjoyed helping and supporting other people, it gave him purpose, so it seemed only fitting that those who adored him through their TV screens wanted to do the same for his family.

That meant I received every version of every message, both from strangers and from the people who knew him the most. At first I didn't even take them in. I knew they were filled with care and kindness; that was all my brain could digest. Most messages from friends said they didn't

expect a response, and that took the edge off my feeling I needed to acknowledge it. There was understanding in that, which I now use in my messages to friends in grief, because I know the weight of obligation in those early days and weeks becomes an unnecessary evil.

As the weeks and months passed, as I started replying to messages or had longer conversations with people, I realised how unprepared we all are to support others through grief unless we have been through it. We're not taught in school how to help someone in grief; it's an almost taboo subject that we speak about in whispers, and it seems we only learn about it when we experience it ourselves. As grief is so present in my life, I feel like people expect me to know all the answers. While this definitely isn't the case, there are important learnings I want to pay forward because I have flinched many times when people have said the wrong thing to me, and have been shocked into silence, had my feelings hurt, or been made angry or defensive simply through a few badly chosen words.

Comments that didn't sit well with me included 'You will get through this', 'You are so strong', 'Some fresh air will do you good', 'I have no idea how you're even functioning' and 'It will just take time'. The two I dreaded the most were 'How are you?' and 'My husband also died and the kids and I have never recovered'. As time passed and people spoke to me about their friends who had sadly lost their partners, I got 'Can you imagine a parent

dying and leaving such young children? That is my worst nightmare' and 'Can you imagine how fucked up the kids will be when they grow up?' Instead of taking you through why each of these landed badly, I'd prefer to pass on my learnings about what has worked and what I do now.

When I started leaving the house for walks, I had a hat and sunglasses on, but I still managed to bump into so many people who wanted to stop and chat. And they wanted to hug me. Each time someone hugged me in these situations I felt worse off, so I spoke to Tanya about this and we unpacked that people's embraces often went on for a bit too long, and it felt like they were transferring their sadness onto me. So in our therapy sessions, Tanya and I came up with a line I could use to keep moving and stay in my own thoughts. I would say, 'I'm having a tough day, so I'm going to keep walking, but next time, I should have it in me to stop and chat.' I would say half the people respected that, but many didn't. Because my grief and mourning were so public, a lot of people felt my loss was part of their lives too, and therefore asked me quite personal and sensitive questions. And they asked them without consideration of the lingering impact of those questions once they walked away back into their daily lives. I think my body language and lack of eye contact were misunderstood as signs that I needed to be helped or fixed, when really they were about being trapped in the confines of traumatic loss and confusion.

When you are grieving you are constantly touched and hugged. I found people touching me in the early stages after losing Jock very difficult, and I didn't have the strength to decide whether to consent to it or whether to say something to make it stop. If it was an immediate family member or a best friend, I welcomed it, but outside of that I simply didn't want it. Now people often come up to me and share their losses, so I find myself comforting those who are grieving. As a very tactile person I tell my hands not to touch them, out of respect for their grief and the tsunami of emotions they must be feeling in every moment. I understand what grief looks like to the outside world versus what it feels like to the person living with it – it looks like silence and lethargy, like a defeated being slowly moving through the paces of life, screaming out for help. And that makes people think an embrace is the solution. But I was trying to find my feet again, alone, whispering to myself that if I did normal things then surely things would return to normal, would get better; I was trying to look forward and see that one day we would be okay again. Someone embracing me took those thoughts away, because it reminded me of how awful Jock dying actually was.

Now, when I have a conversation with someone I haven't seen in a while, or meet someone new, they usually acknowledge my situation and say, 'I am really sorry for your loss, Lauren.' Even though I may have never

met them before, or we might be in a work environment, I find those words very respectful. They don't make me feel uncomfortable or sad; I actually feel more like I can be the real version of myself, since they have acknowledged and have empathy for my situation, and I feel a bit more understood.

The reason 'I'm sorry for your loss' works when people say it to me is that it's one-way communication. There is no expectation except for me to say thank you, which is so much easier than finding an answer to 'Are you okay?' Now, when I am speaking to someone in grief, unless I know them really well, I make statements like 'I'm sorry for your loss' rather than opening up a conversation about how they are. We have been taught that it's good manners to say hello and then ask how someone is, but when that person is grieving all the rules are out the window. Entering a two-way conversation with someone who is grieving or has experienced trauma is difficult and fraught with the risk of getting it wrong, so I stay in the statement territory. Depending on my connection to the person, I might say things like 'Each day does get easier, even if it's just by a tiny fraction that you don't notice' or 'Just focus on getting through today, one step at a time.' A 24-hour period of grief is made up of endless shards of time that when pieced back together resemble some sort of day, so I found that focusing on the next step or the next day, not weeks or months from now, was all my mind could accept.

I have searched for the right thing to say to someone who has experienced loss, for the words I needed to hear, and I know there are none that will ease the sadness and dizziness of loss. I needed to work through the rubble of my life at a pace I could handle, and then rebuild and repair the bits that I so desperately wanted to keep. As I was rebuilding, I had the privilege of so many people remaining connected to me, and I believe that is the answer when it comes to truly supporting someone in grief. My family and friends' concern and effort stretched well past the week of the funeral to a time when the reality of losing Jock started to set in, and I needed support and connection. It was after the initial impact that I was able to use talking to them and putting words to my disbelief as a form of therapy and release. These friends still check in on the kids and me, they ask if they can come out to sit with me next time I visit Jock, they spend Jock's birthday with me, they mirror the way I speak to the kids about Papa, openly and with happiness, and they send me funny memories or photos with Jock. My friends and family walked through the first wave with us, and I am very aware now that their grief was put in the background so they could support mine, and that there have been hard times for them because of this.

Cause of Death

'How did he die?'

I have been asked this question since Jock's death. Interestingly the only people who have asked it are strangers.

While we were still in The Prison we decided that we would not speak publicly about anything to do with Jock unless he had spoken about it in the public domain himself. During the first couple of months after his death I felt like we were being hunted and that the only way to keep our little ones safe was to keep them indoors until the frenzy had died down. The kids didn't go to daycare for months, they didn't interact with other kids, they didn't go to the park or the beach – they stayed at home so I could protect their privacy and control what they were exposed to.

Alfie and Isla still have very little idea of what fame means or how it plays out, but they have been exposed

to it throughout their lives because of Jock's job. When Jock was alive the media wanted to take photos and write stories – but now, without him, when the media focus is on us, I panic. I am a woman with two young children and I feel that I have to protect them and keep them safe. Would photographers come banging on our door at night to get a photo? Would multiple cars chase me when I was driving with the kids? Would men follow me through the park when I was playing with Alfie and Isla? Would cars tail me home from work so they had our address? All of these things happened to Jock while he was alive.

It's easy to forget that interest in Jock's death extends well beyond Australia – *MasterChef Australia* airs in more than 100 countries around the world, and each of these countries has media outlets that wanted to run stories. The thought of this was so overwhelming and scary for me; I had no idea what I could do to escape it or how long it would go on for. I felt defenceless and more protective of our little ones than ever before, and it was also a sober reminder that Jock wasn't here to protect us anymore; that I was alone now, and it was my sole responsibility to look after our kids.

Each person who reads this book will have an opinion. As a family, we have had to survive relentless media coverage, false information, and disregard for our privacy and mental health at the worst moment of our lives. As a result, I am happy to share parts of our life so people can see that we are

okay, but I don't feel an obligation to share Jock's whole life or to breach his privacy in any way. I hope people respect that while Jock did have a public job, meaning our life was public at times, in death he deserves stillness.

I wrote this book because I deeply believe that speaking about grief helps people live with it, and helps those who care for us to support us better. It has taken courage, tears and many panic attacks to put these words down on paper and to share such a personal time, and I am certain that Jock would be so proud of the progress we have made as a family and as individuals. He spoke and wrote of his life experience, without shame, to tell his story and help others, and that is what drove my decision to write this book. I hope that, as you read this book and see what we have had to conquer, you understand why giving Jock peace in death is important to us.

We are real people who have gone through most families' worst nightmare. The kids continue to bargain with the universe for the loss not to be real; as they blow out their birthday candles they wish for Papa to come back; they dream about Jock and then wake up crying as it dawns on them that what felt so real sadly isn't. When we watched the *MasterChef Australia* finale a few months after Jock died, we got through five minutes and then I turned it off. Seeing Jock on TV was so confusing to the kids – Alfie was relieved that Papa hadn't actually died and was just at work, and Isla was instantly happy. So I

had to explain again that Papa was dead and he was never coming back.

It's the kids' innocence and bargaining that makes me so upset when people I have never met before come up to me and ask in front of Alfie and Isla how Jock died. In front of his two young children, with no concern for the sadness they then both experience for the rest of the day. The kids are confused about why someone would even want to know that, and I attempt to explain it to them but can't figure out the fascination myself, and then they get protective of their Papa. I wish I had the courage to ask each stranger what impact the answer would have on their life, but each time I'm in such shock that I just go silent.

When I told one of my doctors that my husband had died, he said, 'Did you marry old and rich? What did he die of?' I had another man ask me if I had nagged Jock to death. A flight attendant in London asked the question in front of the kids, and I get DMs on Instagram from people saying they have a right to know, or that Jock was famous and this is part of the deal when you get paid so much. I have been called a coward for not responding to messages like this. I have been told that I have no right to decide. I have also been accused of causing his death. All of these deeply distressing messages have come from strangers. It's hard to understand how our immense loss could be treated like gossip or entertainment, or why people want to lash out at me because I am giving Jock privacy and peace.

The letter Jock left after our first date, October 2015.

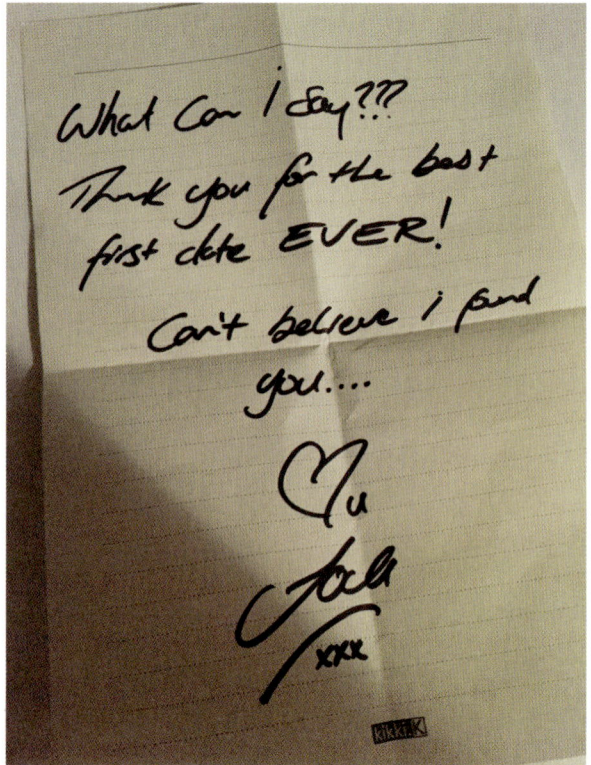

What Can I say???
Thank you for the best
first date EVER!

Can't believe I find
you....

♡u

Jock
xxx

Our first ski trip in Alta Badia, the Dolomites, December 2015.

On our wedding day, Mnemba Island, Zanzibar, January 2017.

Signing the paperwork on our wedding day.

Coming down in the gondola after a long lunch up the mountain on the last day of our honeymoon – Alta Badia, the Dolomites, January 2017.

On our honeymoon in Galle, Sri Lanka, January 2017.

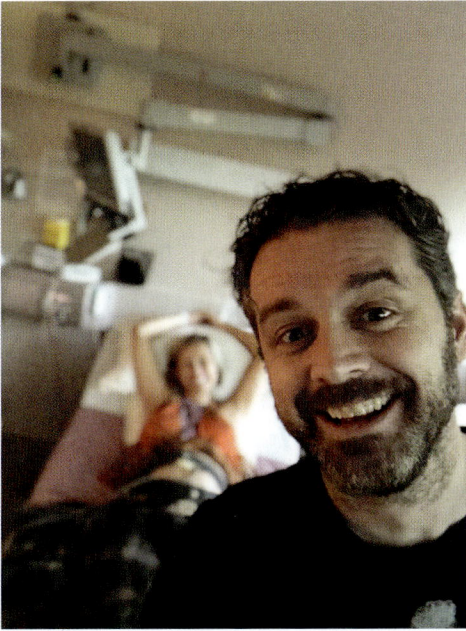

Jock after he raced back from the Faroe Islands when I was admitted to hospital to have Alfie ten weeks early, January 2018.

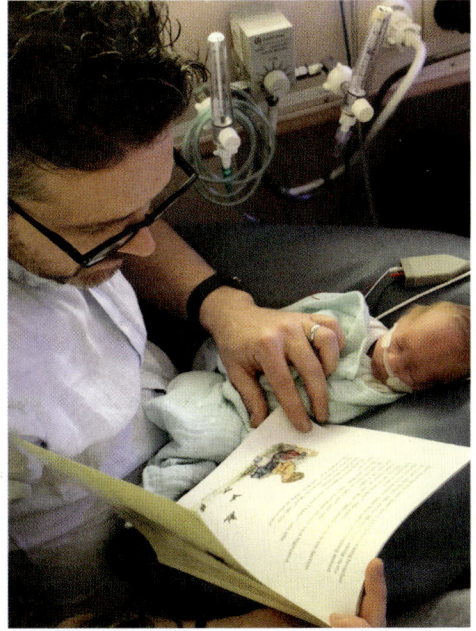

Jock reading Alfie books in NICU, February 2018.

In one of our favourite places off the Amalfi Coast – Ventotene – July 2018.

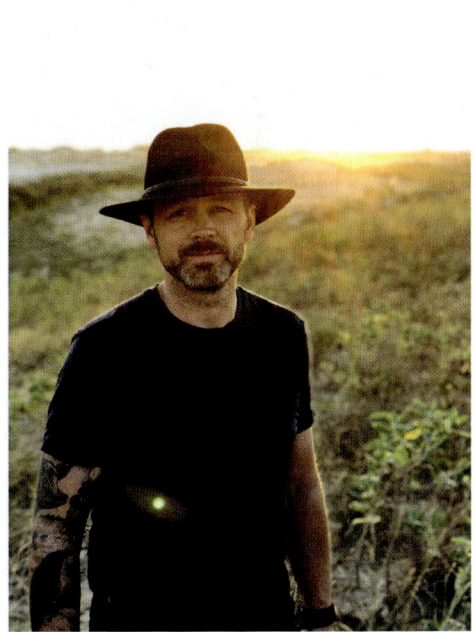

Jock on Nyul Nyul Country in the Dampier Peninsula, the Kimberley, Western Australia, May 2019.

After one of our many lunches at Rifugio Scotoni, the Dolomites, December 2019.

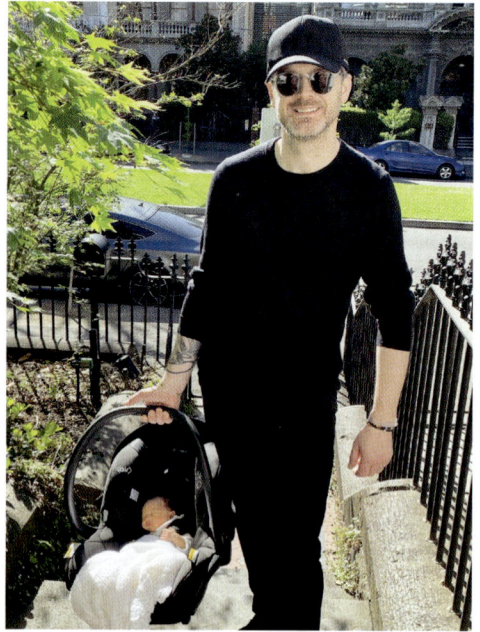

Bringing Isla home to our house in Carlton, Melbourne, October 2020.

Alfie learning how to make coppiette with Jock, November 2020.

On a family holiday with Alfie and Isla to the Gold Coast, May 2021.

Isla's first birthday, which was during the COVID lockdowns, so we did a picnic in the park. October 2021.

In Palermo during our last summer trip to Italy in August 2022.

Jock and our three kids during our annual tradition of putting the Christmas tree up a month early and having a full hot British dinner, in our home in Carlton, Melbourne. November 2022.

Ava coming with me to drop Alfie and Isla at their first day of daycare after we moved back from Rome. Sydney, July 2023.

On our first trip back to Alta Badia, the Dolomites, without Jock, in December 2023.

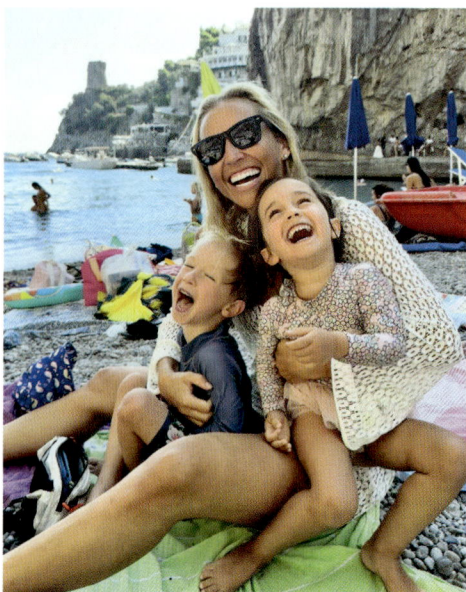

The kids and me in Praiano, Italy. September 2024.

Andy and me after accepting the AACTA Award for Best Reality Program on behalf of *MasterChef Australia*, February 2024.

Alfie, Isla and me in Centennial Park, Sydney, February 2025.

My sister, Lani, with the kids, February 2025.

Three months after he died I was sitting next to Jock out on his grass at the cemetery with my head in my hands, crying uncontrollably. A 50-something-year-old woman walked up to me and asked if I was okay. It took me by surprise as Jock's spot is not a thoroughfare and there are hardly any other people in that area, but also because it's not uncommon to see someone crying at a cemetery. I looked up and responded that I would be okay and then she asked how my husband had died. Jock has no plaque on his headstone and I hadn't said it was my husband; it could have been another family member or a friend I was visiting. I was again shocked into silence, and the woman must have figured I wasn't going to be having a conversation with her about Jock, so she said goodbye and walked away.

Grief was a rapid expansion of my emotional repertoire; feelings I didn't even know existed became part of every day and night. There was no control or predictability in my life, no 'business as usual'. Grief is chaos, and within that, there was only one certainty – Jock was never coming home. As I let the chaos roll out until it eventually slowed enough for me to catch my breath and find the energy to make plans, I realised that no matter what I said or did or thought, I could never change that one certainty.

Seeking, Not Stopping

I went through weeks at a time when I just couldn't stop crying. My daytime grief and night-time grief were completely different and hit at different depths, but both brought my energy levels lower and lower with no respite.

I couldn't figure out how to top up the tank when I was physically exhausted from crying, from having no deep sleep, from being woken up by screams from our kids throughout the night. My body was so unhealthy and screaming out for help as my hair continued to break, my nails split, my skin flaked away. I had chest pains springing up sporadically across the day and night. My body was constantly telling me it was dehydrated but it was a thirst I couldn't quench. My eyes were hazy and not really focusing on anything in particular, with white spots floating across my vision. And my mind wandered

to the safety of denial, allowing me to step through each day like it wasn't really happening: it couldn't possibly be this catastrophic; I didn't deserve this.

Daytime grief would hit me for no reason. I would be pushing through my day and then feel the overwhelm about to hit, and I'd need to sit down and let the tears stream out. I cried in front of the kids, I cried while I was driving, I cried in the shower, I cried when I took the bin out. I seemed to cry a lot in the supermarket – I would stand in the oil section and cry because this wasn't my domain; Jock always chose all of the oils in our house and knew when to use which one. The first time I bought a jar of bread and butter pickles, I cried because Jock used to make ours and keep a steady supply in the fridge. It took away my energy, it wiped my mind of anything else I was about to do, and sometimes it made me angry at Jock for leaving me here carrying all of this without him. Now that I'm not crying nonstop and have clarity of thought, I realise what made me sad in those supermarket moments – I wish I had paid more attention when Jock was alive. I wish I had stored all these snippets of information from Jock so I could keep them in my life and teach them to the kids. But I hadn't and now they were lost.

This loss encompassed much more than purchases from the supermarket. I had watched Jock make crepes for our family every weekend, and now each time I tried, it just wasn't the same. He used a skewer to gently release the

edges from the pan and then flipped the crepe with his hands just when it started to change in colour but wasn't brown. He would use the stick blender to mix the ingredients in a specific tall plastic jug, then leave the batter to rest for a period of time; he would let the salted caramel sauce simmer to a certain level then turn it all the way down. I know the steps, but I lack the detail. It has taken some time and guilt, but I have made peace with this. I see now that making crepes was Jock's thing he did for us every weekend to care for us; I don't have to continue it. I am my own person, I am Alfie and Isla's mamma and I am continuing Jock's legacy for his children by speaking of him with love, by letting my love for him grow, by letting myself miss him and by making him a part of our days so he is with us as much as possible.

As I say goodnight to the kids each night I give them a kiss and say 'Mamma loves you', then a second kiss and say 'Papa loves you'. I have said this to them at bedtime since the day they were born, and I will continue every time I say goodnight to them for their whole lives. It makes me wonder if the universe knew we were going to lose Jock; that this part of my behaviour would carry on once he was gone. The kids connect with Jock when they are resting in their beds and have calm minds; I feel he comes to them in those moments when he can speak to their subconscious and have their attention. I wonder if my bringing up Papa as the last thing I say to them before bed is a good

or bad idea. I am not certain of the answer just yet, so I'll keep doing what I have been doing until I think otherwise.

My night-time grief was horrific, the absolute worst part of losing Jock. It was so lonely, and there was a helplessness in the outside darkness that kept feeding my overwhelm. Night-time grief is solo navigation; no one can help or ease it in any way. If someone were to be there, it would simply delay the onset, not remove it. Night after night, wine after wine, I would fall into the same hole, and I felt like time was standing still. No night was easier than the next, no progress was being made, I simply couldn't get away from the ground zero of losing Jock.

So I started setting some rules for myself, with kindness, as I needed to shift away from the repeated pattern each day and night. During the day I listened to music nonstop to stop myself from getting caught in my own thoughts. I had made myself a 'night' playlist of sad songs or songs Jock and I loved, lots of Ludovico Einaudi. It was self-harm and self-sabotage. A couple of months in I changed the music to only upbeat (but not too happy) songs, and added songs that I knew all the words to so I could sing or hum along. I figured that sad people didn't sing or hum, so if I acted like I was happy, then maybe I could be.

I still have a playlist of Jock's and my favourite Ludovico Einaudi songs, and I allow myself to listen to it when I am five minutes away from being with him at the cemetery and for 15 minutes after I leave. It's a small window of time

where I let myself be drawn into sadness, into pretending our old life is still the same, when crying in the car is acceptable. Any moments outside of that ritual, I don't let Ludovico in – it's too triggering and is a fast track to taking the wind out of my sails.

The first six months after losing Jock I visited him every day, and then that moved out to every second day. I found comfort from being there with Jock; it also meant I could openly wail and feel that it was okay. I'm not sure if I visited him too many times, but what I do know is that if he wasn't in the same state as me and I wasn't able to make the choice to visit him, that would have caused me more distress.

I had to find some control over looking at photos and videos. I would sit in my night-time grief and go back to specific moments of our life together; I would want to see Jock with Alfie playing in the park, or the first time he held Isla after she was born, or photos of us looking at each other and laughing. It became a time warp – I felt like the outside world wasn't there anymore, and I could float around in the land of memories. That made winding down before bed impossible, and sleep a mysterious friend. There came a day when I could admit to myself this was destroying my rest, so I set a timer and only let myself look at photos and videos for ten minutes. As the weeks passed, I then added another rule: no videos at night, because one of my favourite things was to hear Jock's gorgeous Scottish voice.

My last rule was not allowing myself to look at any photos or videos if I'd had anything to drink. This meant I had to decide what was more important, having a glass of wine or seeing Jock's face – but I could never do them together because wine weakened any resolve I had been building up.

I still have these rules in place, but I go through weeks where I'm not able to look at photos or videos of Jock, while other times I stand in front of the many photos of him up throughout our house and look into his eyes almost like he's staring back at me. I carry around our family photo album in my phone every moment of the day, so sticking to the rules has taken a lot of self-control and a decision to prioritise my wellbeing and the need for me to be happy and positive for the kids. Sometimes I apologise to Jock in my mind that I can't look at him just now.

Getting my night-time grief under control was a step in the right direction, and I started to cry less and rest more. The crying was actually making me physically unwell, and I could see that it unsettled the kids. Alfie naturally stepped into being the 'man of the house' and felt a responsibility to check I was okay or cuddle Isla and tell her she would be okay when she went to sleep. In the first few months, I couldn't help but cry in front of the kids; it was constant and impossible to hide. That was part of the learning to live with grief that the kids and I navigated together – that it was okay to be sad, there was no need to hide it, and when we were sad and comforted each other, we felt

better. Alfie went through a stage where he would cry and run and hide in the garage or under his duvet on his bed. This broke my heart. I would go and sit with him there, on the ground, and tell him he didn't have to run away from it, he should run towards me, and I always had cuddles in my arms for him. He quickly realised my arms and chest and neck were places he felt safe and loved, and he runs towards them now, which I'm so grateful for. It reassures me that we're on the right track and that I have created a space that is only for the children, their grief and their confusion.

The lesson of running towards comfort and not away to solitary grief was meant to be for the kids, something I could do for them, but it was my lesson too. As I cried nonstop and they cried here and there, it made sense that their interpretation was that they were meant to comfort me. The one-year anniversary completely undid me, and the nonstop crying started all over again. I saw the massive impact showing my grief had on the kids and it took months of effort to calm their little minds and hearts again. I needed to stop crying in front of the kids, and I committed to trying harder. It's still happening – even when they can't see my face they know I am sad. As we drive up to be with Jock at the cemetery, Isla will ask if I'm crying yet, then she'll keep pulling up my sunglasses while I'm sitting next to Jock so she doesn't miss when I start crying and she can be the first one to comfort me.

I have been out to sit with Jock hundreds and hundreds of times, and not once have I been able to be there and not cry hysterically. I know I am only metres away from him, and I can't shake the deep sadness of that feeling. It's hard to explain, but sitting next to Jock, on his grass, does bring me calmness. I feel like it's a place in the world that is just ours, and with only a handful of people knowing where he is resting it allows me to give him the privacy I want for him in death. Other than me crying each time, the kids are happy out on Jock's grass. They ask to visit Papa and make him pictures or cards; they bring him out Lego or small toys that we can leave for him. They too feel a closeness to him out there that is not morbid or weird, but a connection to him that is just ours.

As I tried to force myself to stop crying, I realised I was looking at the wrong side of the situation. Instead of stopping it, I needed to flip it and begin seeking. What if I shifted my focus and started seeking happy moments and laughter instead of trying to stop the sadness? It was like I was allowing the sadness to sit there on its own, starving it of oxygen and not feeding it. I turned my back on it and tried to focus on the simple joys within my life. It's a brutal metaphor to execute; many times, I felt like I was turning my back on Jock, but when I felt his presence, I knew he was willing me to keep doing it, that he was proud of my capability to move forward with hope and intention. And reasonably quickly, I found that the constant sadness ran

out of steam, that by ignoring it or letting it show up but then not humouring it by looking at photos of Jock, I was pushing it to an outer layer of my days and mind. It will never be gone; it rightly deserves a place, but it's not at the centre of orchestrating all my other emotions and actions.

The year of 'yes' was exactly what this was, seeking, not stopping. I didn't realise it in the early stages of 'yes', but distraction is absolutely okay and soon I felt less guilt about it. It didn't mean I was kicking the can down the road and would have to deal with the full force of grief at a later date; distraction and muting of the sadness meant time could pass, and with that, naturally, the pain eased. I could see that this worried those closest to me – *Is she really accepting and facing what has happened?* – but I think it's been one of the strategies that has helped me safely get to the next stepping stone in life and further away from the impact zone.

Grief Partner

I didn't want to be a burden on anyone. Looking after me had become everyone's priority, and I knew that there's a small window of time after a funeral before life gets back to normal for most people. I wanted to let everyone follow that usual formula. I also wanted to be able to pass off that I was doing okay as soon as I could so people would give me some space and privacy. A day didn't go by without friends and family dropping in; there were also the constant check-ins through text. All brimming with kindness and concern, which I did need, but if there was ever a sliver of time when I wasn't sad, a text would come through, checking in on me, and I would be on a fast track back to sadness.

There's a very tenuous line between wanting to have privacy and being left alone to wallow solo. One is

empowering, and one is isolation. The even harder space to operate in is needing comfort without wanting or being able to do or say anything. This is the domain of the grief partner: their presence gives you the comfort you need without the requirement for a heart-to-heart; they understand the depth of your pain, and do not judge.

Ava became my grief partner, and I'm still unsure if that is fair. She is my daughter, and my primary role is to love and care for her, more so now than ever before. But in her I found understanding. I found a place where we could cry and play together without judgement. We would socialise with my friends together almost as if we had each other's permission to have fun, but also, if one of us fell apart, the other one was there. And we could go in and out of talking about Jock in a way that no one else understood. Neither of us felt guilty for laughing uncontrollably, or saying 'Fuck you, Jock' when we were crying.

If two people in the world understand Jock, get his demons, know the person he was and the person he wanted to be, it is us. It's like his memory is safe between us, and together, we carry the legacy of Jock, his shenanigans, his sayings, his mannerisms, the stories.

As Ava's grief partner, I didn't try to find solutions, and I didn't tell her it would be okay. We would talk, mostly while we were walking on the beach, and the words just went out into the universe without needing a response or an answer. This released a lot of my thoughts, the

ones that formed a large part of my night-time grief, and that release gave me the momentum to focus forward. I had someone I could speak candidly with, an equal in grief, someone I could be completely transparent with. I didn't try to form thoughts; I just freestyled as my words came out and I found understanding in simply letting the words out of my body. We would chat for hours, and I would have no memory of what we had spoken about. It was like the ultimate therapy for me, and walking with her side by side on the sand, the ocean next to us, felt like I had been cleansed of the loneliness for a while. Sometimes I felt like I had a version of Jock with me because Ava looks like Jock, she acts like him, they have the same humour. But she's actually a stronger, more compassionate version, and her intelligence and wit are miles ahead of anyone around her. And just like her dad, when she puts her mind to something, she is unstoppable.

Then, eight months in, Ava told me she was in love with Johnny and that they were moving to London together. They had known each other for a while; I had met him here and there socially, and Johnny was the person who always made her laugh. By the time they started dating, they had built a foundation of fun and laughter; they enjoyed each other, and he already knew she was extraordinary. Jock and Johnny would have gotten along splendidly. My response to this news was unexpected: I burst into tears and couldn't stop. When the tears died down,

I tried to work out why I had responded like that. Over the next couple of weeks, I played around with finding the answer in my head. Did I feel deserted? Was I upset that she hadn't mentioned it to me when it was in the planning stage instead of the decision stage? Where I landed was that it was envy. I remembered that feeling of a big love. I wanted to run to the other side of the world and press the reset button; I wanted to start again and rebuild. But none of that could happen for me: youth had freedom of location, freedom from scar tissue, both things that I was no longer entitled to.

Ava and I are now so far apart, on opposite sides of the world, and we have a void in our little family that stings me constantly. I know that the glue that keeps Ava and me close is those hours chatting about nothing on the beach. Talking and texting allow our relationship to be maintained, but we connect and love when we're physically together. She is the female adult version of Jock, and being in a new place and discovering a new life with Johnny has given her the freedom to be herself. In this version of her, I see Jock more than ever.

I couldn't have found the grief partner I needed in my sister or best friends, and not because the intention wasn't there; it's just that Ava and I are now bound in loss and longing, and that is a special but utterly unwanted bond for us. She isn't my grief partner anymore – life moves on, and the interdependencies of grief need to be released.

She is in a relationship with Johnny, and their love and happiness remind me so much of when Jock and I fell in love. Now hope and future planning are her focus, which is exactly what she deserves.

Medications

A few weeks in I went to see my old GP in Sydney. I didn't know what I needed from her, but I thought it wasn't a terrible idea. The feeling of grief was like a sickness. It zapped all my energy; it made my muscles sore, gave me chest pains and I knew my body was unhealthy and letting me down.

There's a lot I like about my GP: she never rushes me, and she always considers my mental health and frame of mind, which gives her a holistic and robust perspective. Like everyone else, she knew Jock had died, so the hurdle of having to say the words was taken away. We spoke at length; I was probably with her for about 30 minutes explaining how I was feeling and the panic attacks that were coming more regularly. I explained how I didn't need to sleep, had no measurement of time and

no sleep routine, and even with the constant lethargy, I didn't crave bed.

I had recently read *The Body Keeps the Score*, which talks about trauma and how it reconfigures your brain and reshapes your body, becoming a blockage to many of the joys you can experience in life. I had also just finished a book about lovesickness and how after traumatic loss you can literally have a broken heart. I felt like I had a broken heart: it was hurting, I was getting chest pains across the day and night, and it was constantly beating so fast I could feel the thump through my body. My GP and I discussed my thoughts on the two books, how I felt they applied to me, and her medical perspective on trauma and grief.

I left that appointment with a prescription for Valium in the hope that it would get my anxiety and racing heart rate under control. It was for daytime use, more a preventative than a treatment. I spoke to my therapist Tanya after the appointment, and she explained that Valium could have a bounce-back anxiety effect where you take it and it helps, but when you wake up the next day, and it's not in your system anymore, your anxiety is slightly higher, so you take it again. It's a cycle she didn't want to see me stuck in; it's why so many people can get addicted to it. She asked me if I would consider not taking it, and we agreed that we didn't know exactly where my head was at or if I'd fall down the rabbit hole. So, I didn't get the script dispensed.

Instead, a couple of weeks after the initial appointment, I went back to my GP, asked for an alternative and explained my hesitance around Valium. She understood, and we landed on beta-blockers instead to treat my panic attacks. These attacks were what unsettled me the most: when one came on, it was usually during hysterical crying, so I was already worked up, and then I couldn't breathe or get on top of it. I also asked the doctor for some sleeping tablets because I knew rest was a missing part of my recovery puzzle, but I couldn't get there unassisted. The kids were back at daycare, and I was finding that I was having a nap in the afternoons but was not brave enough to attempt to sleep once my night-time grief started. I had taken these sleeping tablets before, so the doctor prescribed them, but told me that all of the medications she had prescribed couldn't be taken with any alcohol.

For the first couple of weeks after Jock died, I was having a glass of wine here or there, probably fewer than I had been drinking prior. But then, for the few months after that, I was drinking every day. I say every day because it wasn't just a night-time thing; a handful of times, I would start in the early afternoon and sip my way through to bedtime. It started with red wine and finished with whisky. I had a babysitter dropping the kids off at daycare and picking them up, so there was no reason in my mind that I couldn't open a bottle whenever I wanted.

I would drink when I was already exhausted, sitting in my mourning outfit, very relaxed on the lounge. I wasn't entertaining myself with a movie or anything, just sitting in my lounge room looking out at the ocean or at the walls. And somehow, the solo time when the kids were at daycare or in bed passed, and a new day began. It felt like I was speeding up my days, and it also gave me the excuse that I needed not to leave the house. I'm not sure what sort of a drunk I was over the period. I know I cried constantly, I talked about Jock constantly, but whether the alcohol spurred that on or not I don't know.

After about four months of this, I began feeling guilty about the drinking. I started only drinking half a bottle and then putting it away, and doing deals with myself, saying that the wine wasn't good for me, so I'd have to skip a meal or eat super healthy to compensate.

One day, Ava and I were going for one of our walks. She only had a small window free until she had to get to work, so we did our usual walk and decompress, and then said goodbye midway down the beach. I thought I'd walk in the soft sand the rest of the way so I could get some more intense exercise in, and then walk up the hill home. As I was walking, a small group ran past, and one of the runners, an older guy, said, 'Join us!' I laughed and kept walking, but he pushed again and said I could just run slowly with him. So I ran to the end of the beach with him and a group of four others. I figured that was all I

would do, and then I'd run up the ramp and head home, but just ahead of the ramp, we stopped, and one of the guys started barking instructions at us, and everyone fell into line. Before I knew it, I was doing sprints, burpees, squats and push-ups. An hour later, I was walking back through my front door.

The group said they were meeting again on Thursday at the same time and place. I put it in my diary, the only thing I had planned for months, and two days later, I turned up again. Running in the soft sand with this group, I found I was at the back of the pack with the 70- to 80-year-olds, and I knew the wines the night before were the cause. I then committed to not drinking on Monday and Wednesday, the two nights before Run Club, so I wouldn't be at the back of the pack with the oldies. We started training three mornings a week, then it increased to five. And before I knew it, my drinking at home had stopped entirely, and I was only having a wine if I went out. I was now able to take my beta-blockers when I felt a panic attack about to land or if I couldn't get my crying under control, and I was having a sleeping tablet if I'd been lying in bed for longer than two hours without falling asleep. And from this came some stability.

I am grateful that my run club drove me to stop drinking every day, but even better, it put me on the sand, next to the ocean, exercising and getting out of my head. The group knew each other, but I was a stranger, so as we did our

warm-up run and buddied up and chatted, they soon found out that my husband had recently died. In that, I found a group of people who showed me kindness, understanding and privacy, who naturally adopted a gentle check-in approach with me each day. Who actually listened, comprehended and responded if they asked if I was okay and I started explaining why I wasn't. Ari offered to put furniture together or lift heavy stuff for me; Yael offered to help with the kids if I needed a break or when I was sick. And Nish shared his mindset on spirituality and trauma.

We decided to grow the group, and I invited my friend Laura. I have been close friends with her husband, Luis, for nearly 20 years, so we knew each other but weren't close. Then one day, maybe a month or so after losing Jock, I bumped into them at lunch and we spent the afternoon together, the three of us. Laura dropped me a text the next day, and we started going for walks and having coffee. Laura is so many things, and in those moments, she was an exceptional listener and showed a passion for life that I craved. Watching the joy on her face every time she stepped onto the sand and looked out at Bondi Beach would make me laugh. It was like she had never been there before – the intense gratitude and joy that it brought her were so innocent. I yearned for that sort of appreciation, but it was like grief had turned the possibility of that feeling off for me. But before too long, seeing this joy five days a week, my mind flicked a switch and I was not only grateful for

the moment my feet hit the sand, but also really proud of myself for being there.

After I invited Laura to join our run club, she was there every day without fail. Her commitment to turning up was for me – I found out later that she had already been to the gym most days before she got there. Fitness, health and being in nature are so important to her, and instead of saying I should get out and run, get some fresh air, or dive into the ocean, she did these things with me, side by side, while she helped me rebuild my health and my strength. We would go for a swim afterwards, then sit next to the beach, have coffee and chat. These chats went on for hours, and I found that the majority of my day was spent on the beach with my run club and then sitting next to the beach with Laura. She gave me company and compassion without me feeling guilty about taking up her time. She asked me meaningful questions. She understood the challenges of multiple children, and of children Alfie and Isla's age. And for two people with lots of friends and family responsibilities, we found space at the top of our dance cards for each other. We also held no legacy friendship so it was like we could start our friendship with a clean slate, but also with a foundation of trust and care because of my long friendship with Luis.

With this daily routine of exercise, coffee and conversation, spending hours outside of the house and near the ocean, I started to feel a shift out of my desire for isolation and constant sadness. Even though it was loose

and unessential, I now had some level of structure and commitment in my days, and it was just the right amount. Laura showed me that people don't need to have experienced grief to be able to carry you through it. She became a student of grief – she listened, she asked questions, she kept mulling over our chats days after they had happened, and she spent many hours in my home with the kids and me. So now I seek out her advice, as it comes from a place of knowingness and proximity.

The panic attacks were also becoming less frequent; however, they were still happening, and I couldn't find the patience or calmness I needed with the kids. A friend's adult daughter mentioned CBD oil and told me that she took it for panic attacks. I spoke to Tanya about it, and she explained how it worked, how to get it prescribed and what some of the pros and cons could be for me. There weren't any cons that I could come up with, so I decided I would give it a go. It felt like a more natural approach and something I would need to put effort into and kind of work with, in contrast to Valium, which I felt would take control and turn me into some sort of a zombie walking through my day with no intention.

My CBD oil arrived, and I started taking a few drops under my tongue in the morning as part of my routine before the kids woke up. I wanted to find the patience and calmness I used to have but that had now been taken away from me. I took it the first morning and got on with

my day. Then I took it the second morning and got on with my day. At the end of the second day, I realised I'd had a great day. The kids and I had been joking around and playing, and all was calm in our new little home for the first time. I know it sounds dramatic and nearly unbelievable, but it felt like my brain had been completely rewired, and I had clicked back into the parent I used to be. It didn't take away the grief, but it did gift me with calmness, consistency in my thoughts across the day and the ability to think and talk about Jock without breaking down. I was having fun with the kids and had no panic attacks.

I took the CBD oil for a few weeks and then put it away for a rainy day. I felt like it was the bridge that helped me to cross over from the darkness of grief to having the bravery to let that stage go and look up and forward. To be able to tell myself that letting go of that dark stage wasn't letting go of Jock; it was simply accepting the passage of time and the relief that it could bring. I take my CBD oil here and there now if I'm feeling a bit overwhelmed or if I know I'm in for a tough day. I'm not sure if it's working now or if my belief in it working is enough; either way, it doesn't matter.

It would be remiss of me not to classify therapy with Tanya, and journalling, as medicine. Tanya has been my therapist for 15 years, and she's never taken a note; we just sit facing each other and we talk. I went to see her initially because my relationship at the time was breaking down,

and I was also worried that I was becoming a version of my dad. About two months after losing Jock, I started going out on Wednesday nights by myself, sitting in a restaurant and journalling. I called this Solo Date Night. I had leant on journalling many years ago when I would do my session with Tanya and then go to Fratelli Paradiso and sit and write until I ran out of words. Many, many hours have been spent at that restaurant, many tears shed, but many epiphanies uncovered. I thought Solo Date Night could be a good practice for me to get back into. I mentioned it to Lani, she bought me a journal, and I started. The thing with journalling was just starting; it didn't have to make any sense, and I was certainly never going to be reading it back, and there was freedom in that. But then I decided to write this book, and my journals became a critical part of taking me back to a time and mindset that I never wanted to experience again. The ramblings of grief, wine and the privacy of never having to say the words out loud made for very honest thoughts being put down on paper. I see now that journalling was a clearing exercise for me; it helped me form thoughts and understand why something was happening or affecting me, and now I am able to pay that forward with this book. I also used a video journal so the kids can watch it when the time is right. I have never underestimated self-therapy; journalling has always been a companion for me through times of unhappiness, and it continues to be a part of my days now.

Jock's Belongings

I have pondered this a lot – whether not having a family home when we lost Jock was a good or bad thing, whether we were better or worse off. In traumatic grief, it's all so chaotic and shit, and memory can be triggering, even paralysing. No doubt, I would have wanted the kids to have the consistency and familiarity of a family home. But the flip side is that it would have become a shrine to Jock. I never would have washed our bedsheets or his dirty clothes; every corner of the house would have been a memory of him and possibly slowed down our mourning. And I know that I wouldn't have been able to move out of that house, which was in Melbourne, not the city I wanted to be in now, and with rent beyond anything I could afford on a single income. But I would have figured it out because not figuring it out would have meant I lost Jock and another round of memories.

Because Jock had packed up our home in Melbourne when we headed to Rome, all the impossible decisions of what to keep and what to get rid of had already been made for me. Now I had to decide where Jock's belongings could live, and instead of having a houseful to deal with, they came in waves, each landing on me when I had different space, financial and emotional capacity. The first wave was the suitcases Jock had on him in Melbourne – they were returned to me the day after I arrived back in Melbourne. The moment they arrived at The Prison, I took them to my bedroom and opened them. I instantly smelt him. Ava came into my bedroom and asked if she could go through his things; I said of course. She sat down on the floor, pulled out a hoodie and brought it to her face to smell it. Jock had been wearing that hoodie only days ago, so his aftershave was as strong as if he had just taken it off. Ava had her moment, then asked if she could wear it; I said of course. I left his suitcases open while we were staying there. My room smelt of him and I could see his things as if he was just on his way back from somewhere and would join us again soon.

I found the set of worry beads he had been using in his pocket, sunnies in his jacket and the business card from his last meal with Andy at Tipo 00 in Melbourne. I searched every pocket for something to make sure I didn't miss any part of him. I opened his toiletries and smelt the cream-paste stuff he used to put in his curly hair.

I looked at his beard trimmer, which still had his hair on it. I later unpacked these suitcases in our new house in Sydney, putting things away in the wardrobe as if he would come home any second and say thanks for getting him set up. I have his bag of dirty washing, his toothbrush; I can't imagine ever not keeping them.

Next the shipping container that was on its way to Rome when Jock died was returned and delivered to me, and I got a package from *MasterChef* with his kilts, sporrans, sgian-dubh and kilt pins. I knew it was coming, but I still left the box next to the front door for a month or two. When I opened it, I found his chef whites, tartan pants and the apron he cooked in. And then, beneath some of his favourite things, I found a box of his worry beads. I opened the box and put the palm of my hand onto them; it was like I could feel him through them, and I fell to pieces. I looked through them, and most of them were original designs, ones he had made and I hadn't seen yet. He was so talented – anything he tried he was brilliant at and he brought his own approach to everything, which I always adored about him.

Every time I unpacked Jock's possessions it pushed me over the edge. I would fall into a deep sadness, sitting there with my hands on one of his jumpers for who knows how long, imagining him in it, picturing where we were in Scotland when we bought it, putting it against my face as if I were lying on his chest again. It makes me feel sick to

my stomach even thinking about it now. But it's the part of grief that tries to find connection, seeks it out, anything at all that can bring back a moment in time that you know you can never truly have again. If I closed my eyes and touched his jumper, it gave me a sense of being dishonest with myself, but it took me to a place that I had taken for granted in my day-to-day life and now wanted back, even just for a passing false moment.

What I found consistent across all of the unpacking episodes is that I avoided them. I put his suitcases from Melbourne outside my bedroom door and walked past them for at least a month. I had to walk sideways to get past them into my bedroom, but no bother, that was so much simpler than the task in front of me. Then, one day a month or so after Jock's death, the day I got his interim death certificate and fell into another multi-day meltdown, I walked upstairs and unpacked them one by one. I discovered a new level of crying, one where I wondered if I was going to vomit.

Compounding grief became something I did from then on – when I was already a mess, I would conquer one other sad task, so it was out of the way, and my sadness was condensed. In those early months, there were no gradients of sadness. The tap was on or off. Now, being further down the road, I have sadness that is better or worse than other sadness. I have explained to the kids that there is happy sad, and there is sad sad. Happy sad is when

I see them being super sweet together, and I get happy sad that Papa isn't there to play with them and see this. Or when I leave a carpark and put the parking ticket in the machine, and remember that Jock would lose the parking ticket every single time we parked. I mean, 100 per cent of the time. Back then, it would really annoy me; now, I laugh and sometimes cry at the memory. And sad sad is when I'm out at the cemetery seeing Papa, or it's Papa's birthday, and I get really sad. It has become part of our family terminology, so I can understand a bit more when the kids are sad.

I see now that the kids have a version of depression or grief here and there. Maybe depression is too strong a word, but that's how I define it in my mind. There was a day when Isla was out of sorts in the morning. I dropped her off at daycare, and then they called me a few hours later to say she was really quiet and not herself. I went to pick her up, and she asked if I could cuddle her when we got home and if she could drink out of Papa's water bottle. She wasn't sick, but those were the two things she needed to feel nurtured and safe.

About six months after we lost Jock, Alfie hurt himself really badly at home. I heard him scream hysterically and ran upstairs to see what had happened. He was holding a long, hard plastic stick from the back of one of his kites against his chest. The moment I saw him, I screamed in terror. Luis was up the street moving his and Laura's car

and he sprinted back to my house in a panic. Laura ran upstairs to me. The stick looked to be impaled in Alfie's chest, and there was blood all over his white shirt. I felt faint; I couldn't think straight. I picked him up because I was scared he would fall, and the stick would hurt him even more. When I picked him up, the stick dropped, and I saw that he had just been holding it and he wasn't impaled on it – in fact, it was his fingers that were bleeding. His hand had been slammed in the hinge of his bedroom door.

There was blood everywhere; his nails looked like they were about to peel off, and all the skin was broken. I had him against my chest for at least one and a half hours while he screamed at the top of his lungs in pain, wailing 'Papa, Papa' over and over. When I couldn't calm him, I asked Laura if she could run to my bedroom and get me Jock's aftershave. I sprayed it onto my neck and shirt, and put Alfie back against it. Soon after, he calmed down, and he finally let us put some ice on his hand. When the crying had stopped completely, I rugged him up in our family blanket – a tartan cashmere blanket we had bought in Glasgow that we used to all get under when we watched movies together. I went to have a shower, cry and wash Jock's smell from me. It wasn't that I didn't want it on me; actually, it was the opposite. I needed him there in that moment, and he never would be again. More importantly, Alfie needed him there in that moment.

Jock used to hate me wearing his stuff. If I wore his tracksuit pants, apparently, my bum would cause bum imprints, and he thought they looked weird when he put them on with his flat-as-a-pancake bum. When I wore his jumpers, apparently, I put boob imprints into them. I now have free rein over all of his stuff, and I have merged a lot of his things into my life. I wear a pair of his sunglasses most days; his jackets fit me, his ski thermals were newer and replaced mine and I use his water bottle. I use his hair product on Alfie. Isla uses his scarves. It gives me comfort, it keeps him with me and it keeps Jock's things in the line of sight of the kids, which they like.

I have also started gifting Jock's things to our friends. The first one was hard because it felt like I was taking something away from his children in the future. But I readjusted my thinking and I knew if I did ever want it back, I just had to ask. I have gifted each item with a lot of thought and only to those friends who I know can handle it. Not everyone is ready to receive these gifts, especially when some are super personal. One of Jock's hip flasks, for example, with his own King's Cut whisky mix still in it, which he used whether he was on the golf course or a gondola, and which I doubt he ever washed. Or one of his favourite Barbour jackets, which had never seen a washing machine. When I gift Jock's things to friends, I consider carefully whether it will be received with warmth or they will think it's strange. I also want the items to be used, not put away for preservation.

With a bit of distance in time, the importance and maybe crazy level of ownership I felt towards Jock's belongings is diminishing. Time has allowed me to sort and prioritise; it gave me the courage to pack items and put them into storage. I now have a small number of essentials, things that are truly Jock, and our kids can have them if and when they want them. These include Jock's wedding band, his watch, his kilts, his Barbour jackets, his flat caps, his worry beads, his cookbook collection, the artwork and nick-nacks he collected on his travels, his Scottish chair, and his beloved Berkel meat slicer and La Marzocco coffee machine.

I am grateful that Jock's belongings came back to me in waves, that I had the luxury of time in which to make decisions when I was ready and that the universe steered Jock to buy things that would last a lifetime. I recognise that the gifts Jock gave to me are now part of him too. My plan was always that Isla would get my engagement ring after I passed away, but now it might be something she chooses to wear in my lifetime, when she too finds her big love. That is bittersweet to think about now.

Regression

Behavioural regression is common for children after traumatic loss, but even though I read about it and was told
about it, I had no idea what I was in for. The kids went back
to wetting their beds, they were tripping up and down the
stairs like they had just started walking, and they had no
memory of how to use their cutlery or which hand to put
the knife and the fork in – these were two kids who had
been proficient in using chopsticks. They woke up at least
five times a night each, at different times, which felt like
I had two newborns. And instead of talking to me, there was
nonstop crying to get attention or because they wanted something. I had to work out what could be wrong like they were
babies again and we were back to wordless communication.

It was tiring and frustrating, and made me a really
angry parent. I had found having babies such a beautifully

enjoyable experience. Jock had said to me that any bits I didn't enjoy or want to do, he would do, or we would get someone in to help. He took the overwhelm of becoming a mum for the first time, and then a parent of two little ones, away from me so I could find joy and purpose in that part of our life. Nights with our babies were precious and peaceful – I would wake up and breast-pump milk for maybe 20 minutes, while Jock would bring me water or a lactation tea (with a cube of ice in it so I could drink it straight away). Then, when I was finished, I would roll over and go back to sleep, and he would wake up our baby, feed, burp, change and settle the baby, go to the kitchen and wash and sterilise all the bottles, et cetera, then crawl back into bed. I was awake for 20 minutes, and Jock was awake for one to two hours. He cherished those moments in the night, just him and our babies, as he found the breastfeeding months quite isolating. This gave him his moment to nurture and connect, to sing his Scottish songs to his little one as they gazed up at him, both falling in love with each other.

But now there was no Jock to support me or to calmly care for our children. At times it made me angry at him for causing me to be a mum – I was never that woman who yearned for children; rather, I wanted to be a parent with Jock. Now here I was, with two young children, navigating this catastrophic period, and then the rest of their lives, without him. There was no respite from it,

they were saying 'Mamma, Mamma' constantly, one of them waking me every 30 to 60 minutes throughout the night. I thought I had reached rock bottom but somehow I just kept getting lower. I was tired all the time, on top of being depleted by grief and my body not being healthy, and I was reaching out for silence and stillness, but the universe was ignoring me. Meanwhile, the world went back to normal as everyone we knew resumed the routines that had been upended by Jock's death – life goes on, as they say.

My brain was mush, and I couldn't work out any tactics or solutions to fix the situation, so I figured I would just avoid parenting as much as I could. I got babysitter after babysitter to look after my kids. Initially it was just for two hours so I could go for a walk in the morning, then I was getting them to take the kids on excursions to the zoo or the movies. I couldn't deal with parenting or entertaining the kids and I felt like this was the best short-term solution. I went out for dinner a night a week so I didn't have to make the kids a dinner that they refused to eat, or teach them how to use their cutlery again, or listen to Alfie repeatedly heckle me about how I was not fast in the kitchen like Papa, or the food wasn't yummy like Papa's. Bathtime was torture: they were so loud and water went up the walls and all over the floor; they would kick each other so one would be crying at all times. Bedtime required multiple books and songs, and then once I closed the door one of them opened it again

within minutes. All these things that we had already dealt with when they were younger were reoccurring, but this time, I had double the trouble.

The kids became a gang and did everything they could to get rid of the babysitter and stop me going out. They would both stand at the front window as I left and scream and cry uncontrollably; even when I was in the taxi driving away I could still hear Isla. But I ignored it, and just kept replacing the babysitter and carrying on. Jock and I never gave in to the kids, and I was sticking with that now, even though their needs and the situation were completely different from when we had made that parenting decision. That was a mistake I wish I hadn't made.

Many months later, in a session with Tanya, she said that I had been avoiding parenting during this time, but now I was intentionally parenting. I hadn't actually admitted what that period of parenting was other than survival and frustration. So when I realised that I had actually tapped out of truly being their mum, the one they deserved, it made me feel sick with guilt. Tanya realised what she had said and also that it was news to me, so we spent the session talking through her observation. Where we landed, and I still agree with it now after reflecting on it many times, was that I wasn't tapping out of myself. I was spending time, as an adult and a woman, with a friend, talking over a meal. Or I was making an effort, putting on a touch of makeup and sitting in a place where I felt secure

to write until I ran out of steam. I might have tapped out of parenting, but I was tapping into myself, and I needed to do that first in order to be able to rebuild myself as a solo parent. I wish I had known that then; the path would have been clearer, and I would have prioritised time for myself with slightly less guilt around my subpar parenting. Tanya said she saw me move from surviving to thriving, and I should feel proud of that, not ashamed.

Seven months in, I had a massive shift – I was ready to be the kids' mum again. It was the lead-up to Christmas, and I was looking at pictures and videos of our previous Christmas, remembering how much fun Jock had bringing Christmas to our little ones. He placed such importance on finding the perfect Christmas tree and placing decorations around the house. Every night the Elf would do more intricate and funny things. He would turn the house into a carnival/circus experience on Christmas Eve, so much so that by Christmas Day the excitement was nearly unbearable for the kids. And here I was, avoiding my kids, not even speaking to them about Christmas or getting them excited about anything in the future. Seeing those photos of Jock reminded me of how much joy we got being parents together, how smug we were that we had such cheeky and funny children, and I realised that they were only that way because of our influence.

It was the right trigger at the right time for me to find joy in that role again, and to find joy in the kids again.

If I was going to be defined by Jock's death and truly continue his legacy, the only important thing in my world was our little ones. I would have nothing, I would be nothing, if I wasn't their mum. And once I got to this point, I realised there had never been a time I wanted to be their mum more than this moment, and I wanted Jock to be proud of the way I did it. So I decided no more babysitters – I would make the kids my sole focus and be with them until we had created our new normal together.

My first step was a star chart. They got a star for doing super basic things like brushing their teeth, or putting their pyjamas back on their bed, or for good listening. They were rewarded with gelato, date nights (going out for dinner together) or Nonna visiting (she was anyway).

Then came the eating/cutlery juggernaut. Food and eating were at the centre of our family life. Every weekend Jock would make endless amounts of food, and the kids always ate what we ate. He would push the roast chicken and vegetable platter towards the kids, and they would use the tongs and serve up what they wanted to eat then pour over their own gravy, knowing the rule that if you put it on your plate, you eat it. Now they were trying to stab their food with the fork turned the wrong way. Tanya said to me one day that I needed to prioritise my battles, and reminded me that no matter what I did, my children wouldn't be 21 and unable to use cutlery. It would inevitably happen, so I should focus on it when I had the strength

and patience for it. She suggested I only make meals that didn't require cutlery, just for a little while, so they could eat with their hands and I wouldn't lose my temper every dinner time.

That evolved into me gamifying dinner – I printed out pictures of different food options and had them on the fridge. Every day, the kids would choose one from column A and one from column B. Column A was sushi, chicken drumsticks, skewers, arancini and fish cakes (homemade, of course). Column B was carrot sticks with guacamole, edamame beans, roast vege chips, corn on the cob and broccolini. Each morning, when I was issuing stars to the angels who didn't wet their bed or wake Mamma up all night, we chose our A and B. Then, when they asked for Scottish pie (Jock called it this – it's just shepherd's pie), I said it was only an option if they used their forks correctly because they couldn't use their hands. And before I knew it, Scottish pie was on the table for dinner, with a fork, and we were on the pathway to normal eating again.

The hardest thing for Isla during this period was when I told her I wasn't going to carry her anymore. She had reverted to putting her hands up in the air and, in a crying voice, saying, 'Carry, carry.' I had done it to keep her quiet, but now I told her she was such a big girl that I couldn't do that anymore, and that instead we would stop and have a kiss and a cuddle. She still tried it on here and there, but then she accepted defeat and moved on.

It only took a few weeks before our little family took shape again, and we were all facing in the same direction. I felt like we needed to get away, have some respite and do something that we all enjoyed. I looked at the options for Christmas – Noosa, Fiji – and found the cost of them was astronomical. Then I thought, what about Italy, the place of all our family holidays? The kids and I were always going to head back, I just hadn't figured out when. Once I put Italy in my mind as an option, it fell into place. My family supported us through our first Christmas without Jock, and then on New Year's Day, the kids and I flew to Italy for our usual ski trip in the Dolomites. The one that Jock and I had done eight weeks after our first date and then every year since.

Italy Revisited

Skiing in the Dolomites was the holiday Jock enjoyed the most, and we had perfected the holiday to the point where we felt there was no room for improvement. It's a real journey to get there – 25-plus hours on the plane, then a five-hour drive, mostly on snowy mountain roads.

I was on a mission to skip New Year's Day as that was Jock's and my wedding anniversary and this year would be the first one without Jock, so the kids and I left on 1 January. Our honeymoon had been in the Dolomites, then all of our wedding anniversaries since. Each anniversary we skied in the morning, then had a long lunch at our favourite restaurant, Rifugio Scotoni, where we ate kilos of meat and drank bottles of champagne. We always spent that lunch planning our year ahead, talking about what we both wanted to do or had started thinking about.

It was at one of these anniversary lunches that we had decided to try for another baby after my miscarriage, and that baby was Isla. It was where we had first dreamt of one day living in Italy or having a family place in the Dolomites that our kids could come and go from as adults. We appreciated that our lives allowed us to make that trip, and each year as we skied out from that lunch we loved each other more. We would ski to the bottom of the run, grab a rope and traverse back to our place on the back of a horse. It was picture perfect, nearly too good to be true.

Flying on that day meant it existed but I was moving. I went and saw Jock the morning before we flew, said goodbye and happy anniversary, and asked where he was again. Spiritually, I hadn't felt his presence in months and I kept asking him where he had gone and if that was it; if he had just been there to get me through the hardest months and then disappeared. I wanted him to show me a sign, something to say he was there. He gave me nothing. The kookaburra wasn't even there that day.

It had been touch and go getting to this point. When 26 December came around, I still hadn't booked the flights. I had told myself that revisiting Italy was a good idea, that I had the strength for it, and that the kids and I had to do it at some point so it might as well be sooner rather than later. But I couldn't commit to the flights. I told myself that I wasn't allowed to leave the house until I booked those flights, so late that day, our flights were

finally booked. That triggered planning and panic mode, which was an ideal distraction from the growing anxiety I was feeling. I started writing lists of what to pack, what work I had to finish before we left and things that I needed to do around the house.

I hadn't been at an airport since I had abandoned our apartment in Rome and raced home to Melbourne. So the thought of the airport, specifically the international airport, filled me with extreme anxiety. We were also flying through Singapore, which is where we had transited on the way home to Jock. And we were landing at an airport and driving into a holiday that Jock and I had always been on together, overflowing with excitement. We had allocated roles – Jock was the bag carrier and driver; I was the holiday organiser and DJ for the drive. But now the logistics of being a solo parent started dawning on me – I had a trunk suitcase, a huge duffle bag for our ski gear and helmets, a carry-on suitcase, the kids' two backpacks and my handbag. And also Isla, who was constantly saying, 'Carry, carry.' As I was attempting to carry the bags from the house to the waiting taxi I realised that the logistics may actually be impossible, but it was too late to change anything.

When we arrived at the airport, I told the kids that if they stood absolutely still and didn't move their feet when I ran over to get a trolley then they would get two stars, and they did exactly as I had asked. As we walked into the

terminal Alfie said he needed to go to the toilet, then Isla said that she did too. *So how do I do this?* I had been a solo parent for eight months; however, I was hardly leaving the house, so this juggle wasn't really in my world. Now I had an overflowing trolley, a couple of kids' backpacks over one shoulder, passports in my hand, and I was meant to run to the bathroom with the kids. Impossible.

That was when I had a little chat with them to explain I understood they both needed things urgently; however, now that it was just me, I needed more warning. When Papa was with us, we could mind bags and the other child, but I couldn't do that anymore. So if they could help me then I would feel like I was doing a better job and we would all get through this big flight happy. They agreed and admitted that maybe the bathroom wasn't actually that urgent, and we proceeded to check-in.

As we walked towards the international departure gate, Isla said, 'This is where I saw Papa last time.' And she was right. I hadn't really thought about the last time the kids touched Jock; they spoke to him every day on FaceTime when we weren't together, but I hadn't put the physical last time in my head. And now Isla, who last saw Jock when she was less than two and a half years old, remembered that last moment. It knocked me off my feet. I had been told by many people that Isla would have no real memories of Jock. But when we were in an environment that prompted her memory, she spoke about it, and she

184

passed that knowledge on to me so I could hold it for her in case she forgot.

I have been cognisant of separating my memories from the kids' memories because I want to understand what is theirs and what is mine. As the kids tell me stories about Jock, I let them ramble for as long as they want so I can hear where their memory starts and finishes. When they're completely done, I ask them questions to prompt their memories. For example, Alfie was telling me about the blue Vespa Lego that he was working on with Jock. He said that Papa had a Vespa; he talked about riding on scooters with Jock. I asked him why he had been given the Vespa Lego and he answered that it was because he hadn't wet his bed in seven nights. Then I asked him how it got into the house, and he told me about how he went on an adventure, just him and Papa, and he was allowed to choose anything he wanted in the shop. He chose the Vespa, and Papa said that was the exact one he would have picked. They had a gelato, and then came home and started making the Vespa.

As Isla was explaining that this was the last time she had seen Papa, she turned to me and asked, 'Why was Papa crying so much? It made me really, really sad, Mamma.' I told her that Papa didn't like being apart from us because he loved us so much, so when we were getting on the plane, but he wasn't just yet, that made him really sad. Alfie then extended her memory with his and reminded her that we waved to Papa all the way through until we

couldn't see him anymore. It hit me that this was the last time I saw Jock as well. He hugged each of the kids for so long, then both together, and then it was my turn. We had hardly spent any nights apart, so saying goodbye was awful. I hugged him under his jacket; he had one arm around my back and the other on the back of my head. We both didn't want to let go; we were both hysterical. We had plenty of time and I wonder if this was a moment the universe gifted us, where we said a proper goodbye. Not the one I would say if I were given a final moment in his life, but it was as close as it could get to that. I, too, kept looking backwards, and the kids and I walked towards the bag X-ray machines, waving and blowing kisses until we had to turn the corner. And that was the last time I saw Jock's gorgeous face.

New Year's Day

The flight took 25 hours, one set of hands and two brand-new iPads given to the children from Santa. It ended up being such a simple trip, the kids were so well behaved and calm. As we left Sydney, the customs officer asked if the children's father would be travelling with us or joining us. I said no. When we arrived into Munich, the immigration officer asked me whether the children's father knew they were travelling. I said yes, thinking that might be the end of it. We still had our Italian visas in our passports, so the officer asked me which country the father resided in, and I said Australia. Then he asked where the father was. I didn't know what to say. I actually couldn't find the words and didn't want to say it in front of the kids. So I said he was deceased. It was a word the kids didn't understand and it put an end to the questioning.

He returned the passports, and we walked through; Alfie held my hand and asked why I was crying.

We got in our hire car and went to meet Lani, Manno and Jakey. They had landed the same day, but were staying a few nights in Munich before heading to their ski village. We ate lunch together and stretched our legs. Manno bought the kids enormous pickled cucumbers at the markets and then I began the five-hour drive to our ski village. As I started driving, I realised just how tired I was. It was now about 36 hours since we had left our house in Sydney, and I had run out of steam. I stopped every half an hour to stretch my legs, which was annoying as it kept waking the kids up, and it was cold because we were now in the snow. I asked myself if I had pushed too hard, if this was maybe too much too soon.

Eventually, after 40-plus hours of travel, we pulled up at our accommodation. I was done, totally depleted. It was night-time, so we had pizza at the hotel and went to bed. I woke up in the morning to Isla screaming with joy at the top of her lungs. She had opened the curtains and seen all the snow and figured it had to be Christmas again! The pure joy on both of their faces was the reset I needed. We rugged up and headed downstairs for coffee and pastries. As I walked into the breakfast area, I saw out the window the backdrop of familiar ski runs, ones Jock and I had done so many times over so many years, and I had that sick, sad feeling. I instantly regretted coming on the trip.

I sat through my coffee, rousing on the kids, asking them to be quiet, not listening to them when they were asking me something, telling them to sit down, to take their feet off the seats. It was like all the progress I had made, all the calmness and stillness I had worked out, all disappeared. I felt so homesick; I wanted to turn around and go back to a home and a life that simply didn't exist anymore. I told myself that I would be going home to a place that wasn't truly home and to sort my shit out and get on with the holiday. Convincing myself of this sounds quick and simple but it dragged on for days.

I went through the paces of enrolling the kids at ski school and getting us fitted for boots. When I was buying the lift passes, the person serving me asked where the kids' father was. I asked why that was important, and he said that they issued one kid's lift pass per parent, so if their father was able to come past, they could issue the other one at no charge. I said he wasn't on the trip with us and I would just pay. As we walked out, Alfie slipped his hand into mine again.

There are moments as a solo parent when some things just seem impossible, like the universe is giving me yet another hoop to jump through. With two children who kept slipping over on the snow, two sets of ski boots, two sets of skis and poles and two backpacks, I had no idea how I could actually get the kids to ski school. I couldn't tell one child to wait in the shop while I ferried the other

one over. So we set off with ski poles pushed through clips on the boots, skis bundled awkwardly under my arm and Isla holding my hand on the other side. We eventually got there; I was sweaty, and my hands were killing me, but we made it. Later that day, a friend lent me a snow toboggan, so I could load the kids and all the gear in that each day and drag them from A to B.

When I dropped the kids off at ski school, the staff asked me to fill out some paperwork, which asked for the father's contact details. I left that blank, and the person checking the kids in said I had to include it. I replied that the kids' father wasn't on the trip and they said it was still important to put his details on the form. So I wrote down Jock's details – I just needed the Italians to stop asking me where my kids' father was, and I figured that I wasn't breaking any rules with this approach.

The kids were now happily back at their familiar ski school, and I took the gondola up the mountain. Everywhere I looked was a memory. Every single moment I had lived before, many times over, with Jock, on our favourite trip of the year. Every day we were excited. Rest days weren't a thing for us – we had to ski, eat, drink some wine and hit the sauna. Day after day on repeat until the dreaded moment when our trip was over and we needed to leave for the airport. We had done this trip before we were married, as part of our honeymoon, while I was pregnant with Alfie, and also with the

kids. The Dolomites had witnessed every stage of our life together.

I had in mind the places that would be really hard to revisit. Seeing Andrea at L'Got, where we had our coffee and pastries every morning, then negronis every night. Seeing Manuela and Christian at Rifugio Scotoni. Lisle at Punta Trieste. Fabio at Rifugio Col Alt. Carmen at L'Fana. Norbert at Atelier Moessmer. All the people we had raced to see each time we came on this trip, who we had shared meals, drinks and conversations with. And who saw Jock and me together at our happiest. I knew visiting each of those places would mean I had conquered this trip, and I made Lisle my first stop. It was 10.30 am, and she did prosecco by the glass, so I figured that was a good idea.

Rifugio Scotoni

Food played an important part in our life, but creating experiences, memories and traditions sat at the heart of us. To say that a restaurant was special in our relationship seems slightly strange, but with all the memories Jock and I shared at Rifugio Scotoni, it might start to make sense as you read this. A big emotional hurdle on my trip back to Italy with the kids was revisiting Rifugio Scotoni. It was the scene of so many memories and celebrations, and it sat in the back of my mind constantly.

I was trying to find calmness now that I was in the Dolomites again. On our first trip back after the international COVID border closures, Jock and I had arrived late, after dark. The next morning, when I woke up and walked outside into the freezing air and looked up at the beautiful baby pink and blue colours reflecting off

the Dolomites, I burst into tears. Jock turned to look at me and I was embarrassed; I literally couldn't hold my happiness and excitement in. We had a laugh – then we had a double macchiato and a cornetto – and went straight up the mountain for our first day of skiing on that trip.

This time around, looking after the kids solo following a day up the mountain, the trip definitely wasn't as calm as it used to be with Jock. The kids wanted to tell me every single thing they had done that day, talking over each other. They had been fed so many Kinder Surprises that they were on a chocolate high until bedtime. So I would finish my ski day in the sauna, pick the kids up from ski school, then we would come home and do yoga together in an attempt to counteract the sugar rush. In the morning, we would sit and meditate together and set an intention for the day, something like trying a bit harder than yesterday in everything we each did, listening when other people talked, or, some days, simply cuddling more. A few days into the trip we found our cadence; we all understood what our days and nights looked like and we were enjoying them.

It was at this point that I started asking myself whether I would be able to ski to Scotoni and have lunch. Maybe I had conquered enough by just being here, and it was something that I could do another year. As I meditated each morning and sauna-ed in the afternoon, I did lots of thinking and pondering. I was trying to work out, now that

Jock had spiritually left me, how I would get on without being able to tap into him.

Then one night, over dinner, Isla started getting a bit stroppy with me. She asked me why I wasn't there when her papa died. Why hadn't I given him medicine? Why hadn't I called a doctor to help him? I answered each accusation as kindly and clearly as I could, but she wouldn't accept my answers. In her eyes, I was responsible for looking after our family and each person within it. And obviously, to her, I hadn't done that very well. I went to the bathroom, locked the door and had a long shower so I could cry with some privacy. I couldn't bear her thinking I didn't care about Jock, that I wouldn't have done absolutely anything for him to have been okay, for him to be alive. It felt like she was being mean to me, and it really hit deep. I couldn't work out how I could change her mind or give her even a tiny insight into how much I love her papa and the things I had and always would do for him.

A few days later, I was skiing by myself, and I felt someone skiing too close to me. I turned to see who was next to me, and there wasn't anyone; I was completely alone. I kept skiing and I felt the presence again. It was like I could see a shadow in my blind spot, and I knew Jock was back with me. I was so relieved and didn't want the run to end because then I would snap back into the reality of him not being there. We had a full conversation in my mind – he said he was sorry that it was so hard, he was

sorry that Isla was being mean to me and not to be upset by it. He told me that he was with us all of Christmas Day and that he loves that I sing 'Caledonia' with the kids every night. Then he apologised and said that it was his heart; he had just gone to sleep and hadn't woken up. I feel like I lost touch with Jock spiritually because he felt it was time for me to accept that this was real. He wanted me to not use him as a crutch.

A day or two passed, and then over dinner one night Isla said to me that Papa was so sorry about his heart, like reeeeeally sorry, and no medicine could have fixed it. Not even a doctor. I have no idea how she would even know to say those words to me. It could only have been Jock. I know he would have connected with her spiritually, saying she should be kind to her mamma, cut me some slack and not blame me for anything.

It was only a few days later that Alfie said to me that I should have taken him to see Papa so he could have said goodbye, but just that first time when he was still there. It was like Jock was screaming out to me that he was still with us and that I was exactly where I needed to be.

So, two weeks into the trip, I had all the courage I needed to make the journey to Scotoni. I did a long meditation that morning before I dropped the kids off, then sat by myself for a coffee and pastry before I set off. The final run into Scotoni is one of the most spectacular places in the world; you take one of those mega gondolas to the top, and then

it's a long, beautiful ski down. Every time Jock and I did this run, we skied next to each other, mirroring each other's movements, until we hit the final run down, released and raced to the end. I had held my shit together all morning, but sitting at the top of the Armentarola run I couldn't move; I wasn't ready. I had my AirPods in listening to Ludovico Einaudi. It felt appropriate for this part of the journey – it was like I was visiting Jock in a way. So I sat at the top of the run, crouched down on my skis in a ball, trying not to freeze, and in that moment Mum called me. I answered and told her where I was, we chatted for a bit, then I said I had to get going. I was freezing now in what must have been at least -20 degree wind chill, and I wanted to continue and conquer this moment. Mum hung up, my Einaudi playlist started again, and I pushed off, beginning the descent.

I saw memories of Jock the whole run. Where we would stop and take photos, where he would pick up speed, where we would forget there was a corner or a drop every time we did the run. And then I got to the final run into Scotoni: I saw the rifugio, I saw the smoke coming out of the chimney, I saw the waterfall off to the right that had frozen into an ice wall, and I took a deep breath and told myself not to weaken and not to fall. I glided to the front door, unclipped my skis and sat on the fence looking back up the run. I was inconsolable. I kept my goggles and helmet on in an attempt to pretend no one was there or that no one would notice me crying. I stopped crying for

a bit, took my goggles off, wiped my eyes and sat in front of the outdoor fireplace while I got my breath back and pulled myself together. Then, after maybe ten minutes of deep breathing, I stood up and walked inside.

As always, there was a queue waiting for a table. I stood in the line, one we had stood in so many times before, and was able to acclimatise myself to the place. Or so I thought. But it triggered me to start crying again, and I was a mess. There was nowhere to hide: the place was packed, and people were pushing past me, asking me if I was waiting for a table or how long I had been waiting, then seeing my face and regretting their eye contact. The line shuffled up a bit, and Manuela noticed me. She saw the state I was in and came and gave me an enormous hug – and in the chaos of a lunchtime at Scotoni, we had a moment to ourselves to sit in the disbelief that Jock wasn't there with us. That he would never be there with us again. I didn't know Manuela was capable of tears – she is one of the toughest women I know – but we were both a mess. Christian left the barbecue in the middle of the rifugio and came and gave me a huge hug – he is a man mountain and Jock adored him, and we also had our moment. Then Manuela returned with a glass of prosecco and told me to drink and stop crying while she found me a good table. For anyone who has had the pleasure of being to Rifugio Scotoni, you know Manuela, and you know that if she tells you to do something, it's in your best interest to do it.

Manuela sat me at a table with her friends – the tables are communal, so you always meet new people – and said she'd order for me. She returned with a half-serve of barley soup, some of their potatoes with speck, and a mixed grill. Exactly what Jock and I would have eaten if we were there together. Her friends were legends, and we spent the whole afternoon chatting and ordering different wines to try. Before we went our separate ways, we committed that on this exact date next year, we would all be there for lunch together again. I walked out and skied down the rest of the run, got dragged across the traverse by the horses, and skied back to pick up my little ones.

I felt a weight lift; it was like I had been released from any more sadness on that holiday. Nothing could be as hard as that. I returned to Scotoni four more times on that trip – the Dolomites had been conquered.

I Am Woman

I truly believe that Jock dying was the shittest greatest gift I could have been given. It's a gift I absolutely didn't want, but without an option to reject it, I ask myself how I can absorb it into my life without it becoming meaningless or ignored. I remember walking along the shore near JT and Bron's beach shack a few weeks after losing Jock and trying to work out how to answer the constant question of 'How are you?' I decided my response would be, 'I've started looking up and forward. I'm not moving but I'm looking in the right direction.' On reflection, I see that this was a decision junction. I could stay looking down, directly at the hole Jock had left, and stand guard, hoping he might reappear. Or I could understand the concept of loss, never truly accept the loss of Jock but intellectually move on. I do think moving forward is

a decision. I needed to have the drive to do it, the courage to walk in the darkness and hope I was going forward and wouldn't fall down too many times. But it was movement, even just the natural and unstoppable passage of time, and that in itself was progress.

What the traumatic loss of Jock has gifted me is a second layer, a second go at parts of my life – and, even better, in an unconventional and free-spirited way. There is no moment in life when you get to press the restart button and redo decisions or pathways. A lot of life and its decisions can't be undone. Some things can never be forgiven. Except in grief. In grief I have been given another chance at the important parts of my life, the parts that I am nurturing and want to grow to compensate for the void that Jock has left. Every corner of my being and my purpose has had to be re-examined, and each time I step forward I do it with intention and thought. I'm not a passenger anymore; there's very little in my control, so the things I can control, I will. Like the type of mum I want to be now that I am our little ones' only parent. What being a woman means to me. Who and how I love. My family. The importance of friendships. It's like the concept of a bushfire: it burns down everything in its path; nothing survives. But, over time, the rain comes, and it washes the seeds from the trees and the bushes. It waters them, and those trees that were destroyed grow back thicker and stronger.

Grief also gifted me a fast track to roads back to places. I am more affectionate with my friends and family. If you started cuddling up to a friend or holding your brother's hand one day out of the blue, it would be weird. But the shittest greatest gift has meant I can do these things, and it's not only accepted but reciprocated.

It has also sutured tears in relationships, wiping out legacy grudges and arguments. It has given me roads back to friendships that had faded away – contact has been fired up again with no conversation about what went wrong or who was to blame.

It has allowed me to pick up the phone to people I would not normally call or even text, and they answer with kindness and care, and a new relationship is formed. I ask for help and I don't feel guilt.

Grief took over every part of my being, erasing muscle memory. Trauma hit me on a cellular level, and I can never be the same again. When I wish I could turn back the clock so that this never happened, I realise that is a bargain with the universe that can never be delivered. And so I don't let my mind go with the hypothetical. Instead, all I see in front of me is unconventional freedom. I respect and have followed the conventional path of meet, fall in love, move in together, get the dog, get engaged, get married, have babies. I have that lifeline with Jock; I am living that lifeline without him, but it is still ours. I feel relief that I am not excited about the thought of doing that with another person. I feel relief that

I can financially support myself. I feel relief that my children have a papa, and he is the only one who will ever play that role for them. And I feel relief that I met the love of my life, and in my heart, we are forever married and forever in love. And that one day I will be laid to rest with him.

This is hard for some people to hear. One friend got a bit annoyed with me and told me they didn't know who I was. That I had a career and a drive before I met Jock, and I should be that person again. I think they were trying to motivate me or shake me out of grief, so I told them to fuck off, but in a kind way.

There are very few things I know for certain about this new version of me, as it's still free-flowing. But the one thing I know without any doubt is that I am capable. Whenever anything blows the wind out of my sails, I tell myself I have pushed through the most chaotic and heartbreaking thing that could ever happen to me, so this new problem sits in the shadow of that. And those who have weathered this storm with me would use that exact word to describe me too.

As I started going out again, in the very early days of this journey, the message to the men in the universe seemed to be that I was ready to get back on the dating scene. I have tried to unpack why that would be, and I think it's that they wanted to be a saviour for the kids and me, possibly thinking that I wasn't capable.

I have an extensive list of reasons why someone would choose not to be with me; each one should be enough to

make someone run in the other direction, but the whole list, wow. I have had a few of my married male friends go through their list of reasons why a man would not want to be with me or why it would be hard to find someone again. As much as I want to be angry at them, I'm simply not. I agree wholeheartedly with each of the reasons they rattled off – some I had missed, so they have since been added to my own list.

Interestingly, a few male friends who I have been close to for decades propositioned me. Each of them explained how they would support the kids and me; that they could accept the love I have for Jock and we would create a new version of happiness and life together. Ironically, I knew all of these guys before I met Jock, when I was single and without any baggage or children, and they didn't hit on me then. But now, with my world in chaos, they felt drawn in somehow.

I watch my friends fall in love; I see the affection and deep care they share with their partner, and I know instantly I don't want that in my world right now. I can't imagine cuddling up on the couch with someone and them running their fingers through my hair. I can't imagine watching them sleep and wondering how I could be so lucky to be with them. I can't see how I could fall asleep on someone's chest and not wish it was Jock's. I know I won't be forever single, but I am still married. Jock is still my husband, and my heart is still completely entwined in our life together.

Unrelenting Firsts

I am a data-driven person, and nothing about what I was going through was factual, rational or had any set path. No data points could be allocated, and no goals could be set to strive for. But I realised in the first couple of weeks that numbers meant the future for me – they represented progress, goals that I didn't need to strive for because the universe inevitably pulled me forward, and small notches that got me further away from the impact zone.

First, I needed to survive a period of time. I needed to get to Sunday, the day after Jock's funeral. I had naively thought it would mean that no more decisions needed to be made and that the phone would stop, but that wasn't to be. I had lost visibility of what else was happening in the world and realised that this day, this Sunday, was my first Mother's Day without Jock. It felt like a cruel irony

that I would have to have one of the many unrelenting 'firsts' so soon.

Jock always celebrated me on days like this, and he gave a lot of thought to every element of the day, knowing exactly what would make me feel special. He was also very talented at gift-giving – he was not someone who would think about it a couple of weeks before or buy something online. Every single present Jock ever bought me, from our first Christmas, eight weeks after we met, through to my birthday weeks before his death, was an heirloom. Every single present he ever gave me was something I still have; they were meant to last forever. One year after Jock had given me my birthday present, Andy said to me that he was relieved I loved it so much because Jock had spent all of the breaks in filming for months working on it. Jock had been sourcing parts of it from all over Italy, having each of them sent over to Australia, tracking them and getting them through customs, to then have it made in Australia, hoping it would be as he imagined. It makes me think the universe made it all work out for Jock because now he is gone I can remember every single birthday present, Christmas present and Mother's Day present from every year we were together. I think that is a rarity and not something many people would be able to say.

On this first Mother's Day without Jock, Andy and Alex came over and cooked lunch for me. They walked

in the door, arms filled with shopping bags, and started their usual kitchen routine, Andy prepping the food and Alex cleaning up his things before he was finished with them – something I, too, always did with Jock. Alex poured glasses of their favourite orange wine for me. Andy cooked me lamb cutlets and salmon; he made delicious salads and vegetables, knowing I had lived off coffee and the occasional boiled egg the weeks prior. I think it was the exact meal Jock would have made me too. For them to do this for me, to cook me a meal the day after the funeral, was really special. But it was even more special to me that they had missed Mother's Day with their own mums so they could be there for me.

I was relieved that this Mother's Day was out of the way, the first of all the first times I wanted to rush through and get done. I have now been through some of the second times, and it does get easier.

I know my sadness is caused by two things. One is that I feel Jock's absence more on these occasions: he was an energy force in my life and within our family, and I feel it in those moments when he's not there creating that specialness. The other is that as a mum, most of my actions are directed outwards and for the kids. So when it was my day, my birthday or Mother's Day, Jock would go over the top. He would write me the most beautiful cards; he would plan things with the kids for weeks so

their excitement built and aligned with his energy, all to make sure I had a perfect day. But now that he's not here, now that it's just me and the little ones, that effort and energy doesn't exist. I don't want others to do it for me; I don't need presents or cards from other people. I want Jock back for those moments.

And so I find myself not wanting the days to occur at all. The Mother's Day that just passed, I ignored – pretended it didn't even happen. I went to the Mother's Day morning teas at daycare and school the week before because it was important to Alfie and Isla, but on the actual day, I had a normal day with no mention of it to the kids. I can see that might sound callous or like I took an opportunity away from the kids to celebrate, but it feels fruitless to tell my kids to celebrate me.

My first birthday without Jock was terrible. I started crying the night before and continued for hours in bed, so I took a sleeping tablet, and then when I woke up the next morning, the tears instantly started again. The kids came into my room in the morning, and without even saying anything, Alfie went downstairs to the freezer, got me two icepacks, came back upstairs and told me to put them on my head. I said it was my birthday, and the response I got was to be asked when they would be able to eat some of my cake. Then they went downstairs and made themselves breakfast. It felt like they didn't care it was my birthday, and that made the crying even more uncontrollable. Then I

acknowledged that they didn't understand the importance of the day to me, and I was expecting a three-year-old and a six-year-old to be Jock.

My friends and family were calling and texting, and I just turned my phone off so I could cry and feel sorry for myself uninterrupted. I was now maybe an hour and a half away from needing to leave for my birthday lunch with friends, so I climbed out of bed, took a couple of beta-blockers and some CBD oil, had a shower and got in an Uber. I called my mum and dad back and said I didn't really want to talk but that I was okay. When I arrived at lunch, everyone was there. Of course, Andy and Alex wouldn't miss being there for me, so they had flown in from Melbourne to Sydney just for the day. When I saw them standing there, I walked up to them and burst into tears, and they both just hugged me until I stopped. They provided a human shield while I reset myself and wiped my eyes, and then it was back to business as usual.

During my year of 'yes', I told myself that if I started saying 'no' it would be like imprisoning myself. Having a birthday lunch with my friends was not something I wanted to do, but I said yes, and then there I was. And from saying yes, I had a fantastic day. I hate being the centre of attention, but having my friends there and seeing their faces brought me joy, and it was a wonderful birthday.

Naively, I thought all the firsts happened in the first year. That may be true for the first Christmas or

Mother's Day, but they actually come in waves each year, and some are freak waves I didn't see coming. I found myself inconsolable at Alfie's first Easter hat parade. I was embarrassed by bursting into tears for apparently no reason, but I couldn't stop the tears from coming. Isla was with me, in awe of her brother, and she cuddled me and wiped away my tears like she usually does. Ironically, the Easter hat parade would have been something Jock and I found funny. Coffees in hand, we would have watched the kindergarten kids wander around instead of listening to their teacher's instructions, and we would have had a laugh together seeing what one of the parents had created from a case of wine. Then we would have said goodbye to Alfie when it was finished and gone and had breakfast together. But Jock never got to have these sorts of days with his little ones. They're often so mundane, times I may not have even enjoyed or would possibly have booked a meeting over the top of so I could have avoided them – but these simple moments are actually so special and so innocent. I wish Jock had been able to experience them. I think of Jock often when I am making Alfie's school lunch. Jock would have loved doing that every day; he would have invested heavily in many different containers and contraptions to make sure that every time Alfie opened his school lunch he thought his papa was a legend.

An agreement I made with myself early on was that good enough was good enough. I made Alfie's Easter hat

so late the night before – after I'd put the kids to bed, tidied the house and got my work done – that the glue was still wet when we went to school the next day. I couldn't figure out how to make the Christmas tree lights work, so they were on the tree but never turned on. And Alfie's birthday cake, which was usually Jock's greatest joy, was an ice-cream cake that Uber Eats delivered during the party. I am not alone in needing to remind myself that good enough is good enough – it's where the parent guilt can creep in, when comparisons with the effort and time of other parents are made. I just keep telling myself that I am doing the best I can in this moment in time.

I know now that there are unrelenting firsts still to come. Isla will have her first day at school, and Alfie will have his first soccer game. I am sad on the kids' firsts because Jock deserves to experience them. I cry because I feel the pain of him missing out, not necessarily the kids missing out. Being their papa brought Jock so much joy; it was really his guiding light, and my mind takes me back to his gorgeous face and voice in those moments he had with them. I am emotionally attached to all the firsts for the kids, and I know that I have been forgetting or blocking out my own. I don't have the answer yet for how to manage my personal firsts or special occasions, like my birthday and Mother's Day, other than knowing they will hurt and not expecting our little ones to be adults and know what to do.

Managing public firsts is another challenge. I acknowledge that I want time to pass so that I am allowed to be happy again and can be the new version of myself without feeling guilty or judged. I recently returned to *Gruen*, a TV show I have been on for ten years. It's a fun show; it's high energy, and we laugh a lot – I mean, the host, Wil Anderson, is a comedian. Wil encouraged me back, and said they would accommodate whatever I needed. He also said that if I changed my mind, it was totally fine, and I could come back onto the show years from now when I was ready. I had worried that Jock's fans wouldn't be able to handle seeing me in that environment or being happy, laughing and having an opinion. When I mentioned on my social media that I would be on the show that night, someone commented that they couldn't believe I would be able to do it. She said if she was in my shoes, she just couldn't. Someone who hadn't lost their husband was saying directly to me, and publicly, that what I would be doing was shocking to her. I had decided to return to the show because that is part of my identity; and it was now more important than ever that I had a solid career because I needed to provide for our two young children. All of the life costs that are usually borne by two working parents – housing, schooling, medical and food bills, celebrations – were now 100 per cent my responsibility. I wanted to scream. Then I realised that I could only move through this at my own pace and without giving

value to the opinions of others, whether they had walked this path or not.

As I move further away from the immediate trauma of losing Jock, the importance of numbers is receding as I shift from basic survival and getting through one day at a time to freedom and release from guilt. The biggest number – one year – is now behind me. Getting to one year was such a big goal for me. It felt like a sort of finish line that somehow mysteriously kept moving. I was continually reaching out for it, trying to bring it closer. I didn't know what I expected the prize to be when I got there; I just knew I wouldn't feel like a winner.

The Dawn

As the sun rose over the horizon at Bondi Beach, and the sound of bagpipes swirled around us, the kids and I, along with my family and our closest friends, huddled in the dark to mark a moment in time for Jock. One year.

We'd made it. Somehow.

The kids and I had painted floating lanterns, and we arrived at the beach a bit earlier so we could light them and put them in the water to be dragged away. Then we sat on a towel on the shoreline, Alfie and Isla each wrapped protectively by one of my arms. They snuggled in, and I felt the full force of my need to protect them and hold them tight. Behind us, in the darkness, our family and friends arrived and gathered against the wall at the back of the beach, there to support us but also letting this be a moment just for the kids and me.

It was raining heavily, windy and freezing cold, and seeing Dougie stoically facing the storm in his kilt, proudly playing the bagpipes for Jock, is an image I will forever remember.

The kids and I speak about wishes all the time, and that morning on the beach, Alfie said he wanted to give all the wishes in his heart so that Papa would come back. I said that it was kind of him to want to give all his wishes but explained that no matter what we did, we couldn't bring Papa back. He said he knew; he just dreams about it when he's sad. I had been doing the same thing, and had been fantasising the night before that Jock walked up to us on the beach that morning, that we had him back and were our little family again. I get the bargaining, the wishes we tell ourselves, and I have stopped allowing myself to do it because it hurts so much to know they will never be.

When Dougie finished playing, everyone slowly walked back up to our house. The kids and I stayed until I was ready to get up. They were both climbing on my lap. They wanted to get closer. I wanted them closer. When we were back at the house, I took the role Jock normally would on the coffee machine and made everyone their coffee orders. A couple of friends offered to take over, but it was a place of retreat where I could be distracted and not have to face anyone, so I wasn't moving. Mark, one of Jock's best mates from Adelaide, and Laura were making pancetta

sandwiches with tartan sauce (ketchup and barbecue sauce crisscrossed over the pancetta) – Jock's favourite breakfast. Harriot was also there rapidly buttering bread. Harriot had been friends with Jock and me since we lived in Adelaide. When the kids and I moved to Sydney after Jock died, she was hands-on in her support – she would offer to come to the house and hang with the kids, or she would be there helping me unpack boxes, so her being in the kitchen making pancetta sandwiches for everyone made sense. Because of how early we were on the beach, my sister had brought Jakey and our friends had brought their kids. It was actually nice to have them there for this, for them to see how we can celebrate life and to be part of that inner circle that helps us carry the grief. Selfishly, it also helped to get everyone to leave in time to get the kids to school.

My kids were emotionally drained by 8 am and fell asleep on my bed. I went to lie down with them because all the coffees were made and I was ready to hide away again. Everyone was downstairs; a handful of people came up to my bedroom to check on me, and I was either asleep or simply wanting to rest. I was willing everyone to go home so I could retreat into unconsciousness and have the day disappear. Isla rolled over and crawled onto my chest, so I spent a couple of hours cradling her, and it was the perfect place for me to be. Later I could hear that Mark and Crissy, his wife, had returned downstairs – they had gone back to

their hotel for a couple of hours to give us some space – and they were now speaking to Alfie. I texted Crissy and asked if she could please bring a bowl of grapes up because I couldn't move and was dehydrated from all the crying. She brought a bowl up to me, washed and with the stems pulled off so I could put them straight into my mouth. Support doesn't always have to be grand gestures; this was exactly what I needed.

Now that I'd crossed the line, what did I feel? Trauma. Deep self-pity. Exhaustion. No positive emotions within reach. In the week leading up to the one-year mark, every hour, I reflected on what was happening that exact time last year, and I started to slowly uncover the trauma that my mind had so kindly buried for me. I can't work out how long my mind gifted me the numbness of shock; sometimes, I think I still operate in that space, but it was a gift in the early weeks and months. It really felt like Jock had died on his anniversary that day, not twelve months before.

This numbness gave me the courage to survive so many moments that could have broken me. That first call from the detective to tell me they had found my husband deceased. Calling Ava and telling her. The flight home with the kids, not having told them the unbearable truth yet. Seeing Jock. Watching Jock being lowered into the earth, forever separated from us. It kept me moving, getting on the flight, making decisions and setting up a life again

for the three of us in Australia. It was a blocking strategy so that I would survive.

When the trauma of what I had walked through started to land, the self-pity kicked in. The week leading into and the week of the one-year anniversary, I just cried. It was an animalistic, out-of-control kind of crying – I hadn't cried like this before. There were days when I couldn't move; it felt like I had been hit by a truck. I couldn't walk up the stairs to my bedroom, so I just lay downstairs. My throat was sore from crying, and I lost my voice. My mind and my body were failing me, and I simply let it happen.

A few days after the anniversary it was my dad's birthday. I texted him saying I would call him later in the day with the kids. I didn't have the energy to, and the kids were physically hanging off me 24/7, so I didn't end up calling him. A few days after that he texted me saying I had enough time to post on social media but not enough time to wish my own father a happy birthday, how lovely of me. The post I had put up was a tribute video to Jock on the anniversary. I haven't had contact with my dad since.

I was kind to myself – I had naps while the kids were at school and daycare, I meditated, I visited Jock every day, I drank miso, I had a massage, I did sound therapy and some crystal healing thing, I went to bereavement yoga, I talked to Tanya, and I didn't drink. I took beta-blockers to give me some rest from the crying, and sleeping tablets each night so my mind could take a break. I tried not to

be angry with myself, ashamed that I wasn't being strong. Now I really understood the burden of grief.

I do feel ashamed though that the kids were knocked for six by seeing me like that. This was the period when I made most of my mistakes, and I have been really angry at myself ever since. I know that none of them were made from a place of intention or recklessness; I just couldn't cope with the trauma and memory of it all. Off the back of this, it felt like it had just dawned on the kids that Jock was actually dead. I found Isla crying in her bed at night, and as I cuddled and rocked her, she said, 'I love you, Mamma, but I need Papa.' Our precious little four-year-old daughter was feeling loss and grief, and there was nothing I could do to take that away for her. Alfie wanted something of Jock's on him at all times, and would tell me a story that Jock gave it to him because they're best friends. Both the kids bit their nails down – they'd never done that before. And I found Alfie speaking in a low voice to Jock, telling him stories of what he'd been doing and asking, 'Are you proud of me, Papa?'

It's not that their behaviour was regressing again, but their hearts were broken, and they understood loss and longing now.

Getting It Wrong

Immediately after the one-year mark, the kids' behaviour started shifting into patterns that initially seemed sweet, until I realised they actually came from a place of pain and yearning. If I were to look at a list of self-assessments to see where I got it wrong and what I wish I could undo, a lot of things from this period would feature on that list. What makes me even angrier at myself is that they came at a time when I should have known better, I should have been more in control of my emotions, and I should have had greater insight into the kids' version of grief and how I could trigger or support them. I know that sounds like I'm being hard on myself, but I can say I am proud that I could see the problems quickly and find a remedy immediately. Are my kids forever scarred? No. But would I have preferred their little hearts not to have to feel any more pain and sadness? Yes.

One of these regrets involves the way I set up the house for the one-year anniversary. On our dining table, I had put pictures of Jock with the kids, a big vase of thistles, which the kids know is Papa's flower, and one of the stag candle holders we had bought in the Scottish Highlands. I had thought I'd have it there for the day when everyone came to the house. But I liked seeing Jock's face each time I walked past the table or when we ate a meal, so I left them on the table for maybe a week or two. Each day I would light a candle and put it on the stag candle holder, my version of Jock's Yahrzeit candle, and it burned day and night.

Since the photos were on the dining table, the kids started setting the table for four each night, so Papa had somewhere to sit. The first night, I looked at our two little children being so considerate of Jock, and it melted my heart. But then this developed into arguments about who got to sit next to Papa's spot, why I was sitting in Papa's Scottish chair because they wanted Papa to have it back, and why I didn't put a plate on his placemat. So one day, when they were at school and daycare, I took the photos off the table and packed away the stag candle holder.

The first night, Isla had an epic meltdown and was screaming at me, pointing her finger, saying that it was her papa and demanding I put the photos back 'right now!' She was hysterical. But above all, she was angry at me, and

I burst into tears. This sent her into a confused tailspin, and she started crying. I had no idea what to do or say, so I told them they could eat whatever they wanted for dessert – they both had Tunnock's Caramel Logs. Then, out of guilt, I said they could watch some TV before bed. As we watched TV, me in the middle with an arm around each of them, family blanket over us, I silently asked for forgiveness.

The next day, I spoke to Tanya, who explained that what I had done was okay and suggested I explain to the kids that the photos and candle were part of the ritual of marking one year, and that I had just returned the photos to their forever place on the shelves. Maybe they hadn't noticed all of the photos around the house. So I held their soft little hands and took them for a walk around the house, pointing out each photo and telling them the story behind it. All of the frames are double-sided and have a photo on the back too, so I told them we could flip it around whenever we wanted, and we'd have a new photo. They thought I was brilliant and possibly had invented the double-sided frame. The crisis was minimised; they were distracted by the photos now in their forever places, and the dining room shrine set-up wasn't talked about again.

Another thing that comes to mind is the kids' albums. My mum had printed out small albums for each of the kids, filled with beautiful photos of them with Jock. She gave them to the kids after the dawn service. It was such a

thoughtful idea. But then, whenever we went out for dinner and I said they could take one toy and one colouring-in book, they grabbed their 'Papa photos'. No toy, no colouring-in book; they just wanted to look at photos of Papa. Each time they did that, one of them would go quiet, and after a bit of a cuddle with me at the table, they would say they were sad. Most of the time, they would show the waiter or, even worse, in more than one instance a friend of ours who owned the restaurant and was close to Jock, and say that their papa died.

The albums were just too much to handle when we were out having dinner. So I explained that I got sad too sometimes when I looked at photos, so we'd keep them at home and not bring them out when we were having fun at dinner anymore. I packed them away when we got home, and they never asked for them again. I should have known that if I got sad when I looked at them, of course they would too – such an oversight.

And then there were the slippers. I have been wearing a lot of Jock's things, so when the weather turned cold, I pulled out the Glerups slippers he used to buy in Copenhagen. I never liked these slippers: he always bought them a few sizes too big, on purpose, and he shuffled around the house all winter. He would buy a new pair in exactly the same colour and style anytime he went even close to Denmark, and they're not the sort of slippers that wear out so we have quite an extensive collection of the

same shoe. The night I put a pair of Jock's slippers on and something flicked in Alfie. To preface this, Alfie is an angel child – super adorable and thoughtful, with extremely high emotional intelligence. Alfie became so angry at me, it was like he had no control over what he was saying or doing. He told me to take them off as Papa had bought him a matching pair because they were best friends, and I wasn't allowed to wear them; they weren't mine. Isla ran to her wardrobe and retrieved the miniature pair Jock had bought for Alfie, which she had inherited once he grew out of them. Isla thought she was helping; instead, Alfie lost his shit even more comprehensively.

Hours later, I had one of Jock's flannelette shirts on, and Alfie crawled on my lap for a cuddle. In that moment, I realised it was Jock's shirt, and thought it had upset him, but he just told me that he loves it when I wear Papa's clothes. It was a confusing couple of hours for me, but I realised later that in their little minds there are fractions of difference within actions. On reflection, it makes absolute sense that Alfie was affected by the slippers. Being Papa's best friend was a special role that Jock created for him, and I needed to nurture that space and let it remain his place for his memories. The slippers were packed away.

I've been tormented by how much emotion or rawness I should show in front of the kids. Should I try not to cry in front of them? Should I save telephone calls for when

they're out of earshot? I initially decided that I was going to be completely open with the kids, softening the heavy stuff but not hiding it. I'm not sure if that was intentional or because that's all I was capable of. For months now, I have told myself that I will not cry in front of the kids. I have said to myself that enough is enough, it isn't normal to see your parents crying when you are a kid. I also don't want them to think that my sadness is a dark cloud that hangs over me or our lives, and have them alter their behaviour to accommodate that.

I have also found comfort in their touch when I'm crying. So if they come to cuddle me, I give them a big cuddle and cry even more. I don't want to do that anymore. I don't think it's fair for them to feel that helplessness or that they are responsible for looking after me.

We went to visit Jock, and after I pledged not to cry, I didn't. It took 18 months and many hours spent sitting out with Jock, and I told myself that I had to try really hard not to cry. I sat on the grass next to Jock's head and immediately felt the sadness wanting to creep in. So, I started weeding his grass. I felt Jock laughing at me, with me – this was the most gardening I had ever done. I said back to him that these were the lengths I would go to not to cry this one time, but to know that I loved him today more than ever before.

I found my support in our little ones, and I knew I needed to find mental health support for them, but either

the psychiatrist or psychologist didn't do bereavement work with children, or their waitlist was years long. The kids now have regular sessions at the National Centre for Childhood Grief in Sydney, and their approach is open-plan play-based therapy, which Alfie and Isla respond really well to. When we arrive for our sessions, the kids play and I sit with their therapists on a couch or the floor next to them, and we have a conversation in front of Alfie and Isla so they know what's going on. They don't take me to another room so we can do secretive adult stuff – everything we talk about is out in the open. Then at the end of the session their therapists debrief in the same position and within earshot of the kids so everything is transparent. I want Alfie and Isla to trust in me and know that I won't betray their privacy or confidence, or say anything that might make them feel embarrassed.

It has also been a place of support for me personally. I can call either of their therapists any time I have a question, which happened in the lead-up to a Father's Day breakfast at Alfie and Isla's daycare less than six months after Jock had died. I didn't know whether I should go or whether Joel or my mum should go, or what the other options could be. Alfie's therapist said I should do whatever would make them feel special. So Ava and I went, and so did Joel, JT and Bron. The kids had a wonderful time, and it was another layer of reassurance from those closest to them that they were cared for and considered.

As part of the ritual of going to their sessions, they can decide if they want to drop in to JT and Bron's house to say hi, which is a short drive away, and if they want to stop and see Papa on the way home. I will never force them to visit Jock, and if one of them wants to go and the other doesn't, we have an agreement that they can just sit in the car. That has only happened once, and it was because Isla was asleep. When she woke up ten minutes after we'd left, we had to turn around and take her back so she could say goodbye to Papa.

After their last session, we went to see Jock and as we drove into the cemetery Isla said from the back seat in a voice that sounded like she was rolling her eyes, 'And now here comes the sad bit.' I asked her what she meant and she said this is where I started crying every time. I asked how we could make it fun and Isla suggested we tell Papa funny stuff, so she was going to tell him all of her teeth had fallen out. Alfie said he would tell Papa that since his two teeth had fallen out he could only eat soup. They thought these were fantastic, and we all got out of the car laughing. The kids ran towards Jock's grass so they could start sharing their funny stories. Isla sat and rested her back on Jock's headstone and said she was going to sit on Papa's head today because he would find that funny. Alfie lay down on Jock's heart, the place where he always sits or lies. They told Jock their funny stuff, and Alfie whispered into the grass that Isla was

telling Papa porky pies (a term Jock would have used). We all had a giggle, they both sat between my legs, Alfie leaning back on my chest, Isla in between his legs and leaning back on his chest like we always do, and we had a long family cuddle, then Isla pulled my sunglasses off my face to check that I hadn't been crying (I hadn't!). The three of us sang Jock 'Caledonia', then we said goodbye and got into the car. No tears were shed. A corner had been turned.

I had found it hard to explain to the kids why I couldn't control my crying when I visited Jock. I also found it difficult to explain my overwhelm at parenting them solo. I have stopped telling them 'I am doing the best I can' or 'I can only do so much at once'. And I have said 'I am about to lose my shit' a few too many times. I know this because Isla repeats these phrases back to Alfie as a word of warning – 'Alfie, if you don't give me the tennis racket, Mamma will lose her shit.' The fact that I'm a solo parent doesn't make me unique. There are plenty of solo parents around the world, and parents in general, who want to say those words. I can think them, but I don't want to say them to the kids anymore.

I don't want their recovery to include recovery from my parenting flaws. I want them to see me trying and know that I am not defeated, that it's our version of what is possible, and that their mamma is capable. At some point in their lives, I want them to ask themselves or

each other, 'How did Mamma do it?' And I want their answer to be, 'Because she's a fucking legend.' It's worth striving for.

I want them to see me for the wife, woman and mother I am. And to see the impossible task that was in front of me that, together, we made possible. This is when they will see me as human, they will see what loving someone by choice looks like and they will understand how hard I tried to dam the tsunami of grief that I didn't want to touch them.

Intentional Parenting

In the first year, parenting was hugely challenging. Patience showed up very rarely. Alfie and Isla were all-encompassing and demanding, and they didn't allow me time for anything other than giving them my full and undivided attention if we were in the same building. I reflect on the mum I used to be before our loss – I rarely got frustrated with the kids or raised my voice. After Jock passed, I felt like I nagged and disciplined them every waking moment.

The kids talked *at* me nonstop, and I mean that even when they were in bed, they were yelling, 'I love you so much, Mamma!' and if I didn't respond, one of them would cry. They talked at me so much in the car that I eventually made a deal – they could speak to me during one song, and then during the next song I would have quiet time. We also had an agreement that they would say

when they'd finished talking so the other one would know they could start talking straight after. It was relentless, and the constant talking took away any energy I had left in the tank.

Whenever I wanted to do anything – make a call, respond to a text or think about something – they would jump in with even more gusto to get my attention. It made working while they were awake impossible. And they would yell out to me whenever they thought I had escaped for a minute – when I was in the shower, they would come in and talk at me; when I took the bins out, they would follow me. It was mental. And somewhere between all that, I was meant to be writing this book.

Unfortunately, as I lost my patience, I lost my shit. I raised my voice with the kids on a daily basis, and I had never done that before. I tried to unpack what was triggering me and then work backwards from there to find a solution, because I felt like my nerve endings were fried. As I was writing this, Isla crawled onto my lap and said she just wanted to watch me. She went to bed an hour ago. She was snuggled into my chest, and every minute or so she asked me a question – 'What are you doing?' 'Why do you type so loud?' 'Can I wear my helmet?'

Working through this in therapy, Tanya and I came to one firm conclusion – this is my life. I am a solo parent, trying to work and find calm so we can all operate together cohesively. When we broke it down, it was me getting angry

and having a short fuse that I wanted to stop. It was the only thing about the whole family dynamic that needed fixing. If I got that under control, then everything else sang.

We worked out that I would get pushed to the edge when one of three things happened – loud noises, yelling, or inaction. I would be so on edge that if someone dropped cutlery or a glass in a restaurant, I felt it in my body like someone had fired a gun next to me. My kids would yell at me constantly when they were upstairs and I was downstairs. When I was trying so hard to be present and make them feel heard, this was exhausting. I could never finish what I was doing because I'd hear them yell out, walk to where they were and ask them to start again because they now had my full attention. And when I was trying to juggle this new solo parenting role and running late, or trying to hustle them to the car while carrying more than I was able to, they'd move at a snail's pace (also known as an average child's pace). This exercise of working out my triggers was so enlightening it immediately made me feel better just having the clarity.

From there, I have established an approach to circumvent these triggers and parent intentionally. I have fallen off the wagon and lost my shit here and there, but for the most part, everyone is happy with the guardrails. We have agreed that if we want to speak to each other, other than when I'm driving, we need to have eye contact – no yelling from different rooms. I get up super early and I'm organised

before the kids wake – gone are the days of all of us getting ready to go out at the same time. I sort myself out before the kids so that I am there to help them or keep them from the distraction of toys or books instead of getting dressed.

Loud noises I don't have an answer to just yet. One day, we arrived home from the usual school and daycare pickup, and Alfie slammed our back metal gate shut behind him. I jumped out of my skin, turned around and yelled, 'Get into time out NOW!' Alfie sat down exactly where he was standing. Usually, he would ask where he should do time out and drag his feet a bit; this time, he saluted into position. I walked inside, hated on myself for a few deep breaths, then went outside and apologised to Alfie. I tried to explain that loud noises frighten me more than normal, and if he could not slam the gate again like that, I would appreciate it.

In my session with Tanya that week, she told me to go out and slam the gate as many times as I could. She said I would never get used to the loud noise, but I would see that nothing in the world changed or was impacted; it was simply a loud noise.

Intentional parenting is probably something lots of calm parents already practise. But for me, for my little family, our dynamic and way of operating was completely broken and I realised that we had all gone into survival mode. Now I wanted to intentionally rebuild and figure out the relationship between me and each of these innocent little

individuals who are evolving every day, and then between us as a family of three. I alternate who I drop off or pick up from school or daycare first so I get time with each of them individually every day, we eat dinner together every night, I sing them their own song each night, I cuddle them and have little whisper chats with each of them as I put them to bed. And we have special things that are just ours. Alfie and I share a look between us when Isla says something ridiculous like 'I'm a queen, and I'm sending you two to jail!' – we roll our eyes and shake our heads. Isla and I like to share a pinky promise when no one else can see.

It's in the bedtime whisper chats that the kids really talk to me. Isla said to me the other night, 'This is a very sad thing to say, Mamma, but I'm sorry Papa died, and that makes you cry.' Alfie tells me he likes it when I put my hand on his cheek and leave it there. It's warm, and he enjoys that feeling.

One of the downsides of my avoidant parenting stage was that the people around me stepped in and did some parenting of my children. And once they started that it has been very difficult to make them stop. It also made me feel like they didn't view me as a capable parent, and resentment started to mutually build. Alfie and Isla were being disciplined, even screamed at, and I didn't have the courage or strength to ask in those first few weeks for it to stop. I almost felt like I had to just take what I could get

when it came to help with the kids. I admit that I lost my shit once when two people were raising their voices at the kids – I screamed at them to stop yelling at my kids, that they had just lost their dad. I have since made a commitment to myself that I would be more like Jock – I would protect our kids without feeling guilty or uncomfortable about it, and I would stand strong with my own personal boundaries and not let any be breeched.

I know the progress the kids and I have made is super basic, but I can see Alfie and Isla respond when they feel safe. Safety means clear communication from me, boundaries, rules, agreements that we all buy into. And a star chart, of course.

Living with Urgency

I decided that life was going to be extraordinary; it was the only way that grief could be drowned out. I had read a lot of different perspectives on grief – for a while, I clung to the concept that grief takes up 100 per cent of your life, so you have to build a bigger life to make it a smaller percentage. I like data points, so this idea resonated, and I could picture it. But then I started shifting my focus to seek happy moments and laughter instead of trying to stop the sadness, and that seemed more of a gentle and emotional way through grief.

I now operate in a world where I know extreme darkness. I understand that bad things can happen and chaos is left in the aftermath. Sadly, I think I now know the extremes my mind and body can be taken to when catastrophe strikes, and in moments when I reflect on that

I feel helpless and weak, whereas at other times I only see my strength and resilience. From that knowledge, I now have a choice as I move through life: either allow myself to expect the worst, or take the view that the universe has its own balance sheet and I am owed big time. I prefer the latter. I have been forged by the flames, and as I emerged out the other side, I found there were parts of me that the flames had melted away and other parts that can never be taken from me. Anyone who has to walk this path has a different experience; my experience has been completely life-altering. I was forced right to the edge, then I turned around and walked away.

The first year after losing Jock, I was in a complete daze. I was easily distracted, my memory was shot and time was of no importance, which meant I got absolutely nothing done. I set no goals and didn't try hard at anything. Bron had suggested a book to me about having faith in something other than yourself. It was about releasing blocks in your life and finding purpose again, and it had tactics I could use when I was feeling the overwhelm of it all. As I read the book, every part of it landed. Meditation was a major focus and even before I had finished the book I had started the practice.

The old version of me was a person of habits; I needed structure and predictability to my days so I could fit everything in. But now, I had lost all order in my life and there was nothing I habitually did each day – I just rolled with

240

the punches. And from that I grew anxious without realising the cause. I didn't set an alarm; I figured one of the kids would wake me, and they were both at daycare, so there was no official start time. I think about this now and shake my head. We just slept until we woke up? Who does that? I realised from reading Bron's book that I needed meditation to be part of my daily habit, so it became the first thing I did each day. Meditation forced my hand into setting a routine because if I didn't get in front of the kids and do what I needed to before they woke up, then meditating wouldn't happen. I also had to wake and meditate because the depressive mind, the sadness, had the ability to take over once my mind was active, so it slowed that process down. Sometimes meditation didn't even allow the negative to latch on. Then, before I knew it, a habit was born, a daily alarm was set, and I was doing something just for me in the silence of the morning.

From that practice, I felt my inner power reignite. My sense of strength and purpose began a slow rebuild, and soon, I felt like I was able to radiate that. I'm not sure if I would have been as open-minded about this without my recent spiritual journey or if my mind allowed me to imagine anything if it meant I was coping – another thing I will never know the answer to. This first step in my day was such a contrast to what the previous months had held – being woken with a start by a child screaming from their room or right next to my bed. That never set my day up

for success. Now I had control of the way I woke up and of my first step of the day, and that cleared a lot of the hard-done-by debris that I felt was in front of me every day. I was no longer a victim in any way.

Feeling a small sense of empowerment in my day allowed me to set about curating a new life of the usual things we would do as a family, and new experiences that were now just the kids' and mine. It's a delicate mix, on one hand, of not moving away from our family memories and rituals and, on the other, not dwelling on the sadness of those memories. I think this process showed the kids that we were moving, we were progressing and growing. They love adventure and new things; they love our little family meetings where we huddle and thrash out something together, making them feel like they are part of the decision-making. And I found as we had more of these family huddles, as I involved them in planning and ideas, the more we moulded into our new version of a family. They had more childlike enthusiasm for the everyday; were excited that we were playing a game together. The fun and light-heartedness was coming back to us.

One Solo Date Night, I was journalling about this new dynamic. I was trying to analyse what I got from it other than seeing joy in the kids, which is a fast track to happiness for me. But was I acting? Was I genuinely in this with them? Was I really excited about planning for the future, or was it just a distraction? And so I wrote about what it

would mean if I was living with urgency. It didn't mean rushing, and it didn't mean living like every day was my last. To me, it meant having an appreciation for my life and not wanting to leave anything behind. I wanted to dream of something again and then actually do it. And I wanted for my kids to look back at their life, see the catastrophic hole that Jock left, and shake their heads at how full and meaningful their life was. The thought of Alfie and Isla being adults and reflecting on a wonderful life, well-lived, gave me the motivation and energy to live with urgency.

This new perspective changed everything. Living with urgency made me feel like I had turned a corner and now had a clear path towards something bright. I was drawn to that light, and could feel love and joyfulness in a way that I hadn't been able to before. This second layer, or second approach at life, made everything more visceral and more real. The dress rehearsal was over, and this was now the performance of my life. I made intentional steps, and valued my time and mindfulness more than ever.

I also realised that I was all our children had now. My influence, my behaviour and my livelihood are all critical to their survival in life and in the way they will build towards adulthood. Living with urgency meant I was not allowed to fuck this up for them.

That realisation made me pencil in three months in Italy. I could take Alfie out of school for a term and the kids

and I could spend that time back there. I couldn't come up with one reason why this was a bad idea and so, unlike the ski trip, my planning commenced. In moments of doubt, I took my mind to the image of Alfie and Isla as adults reflecting on a life well-lived, and I pushed on with the planning. A part of me also wanted to interrogate the idea of Italy as our permanent home again. We had made that decision as a family before Jock died, and I wanted to see if it still had buoyancy. I asked myself if I was pushing myself too hard, if I was testing how strong and capable I actually was, and if I was attempting the impossible to prove something to myself or to others. Losing Jock had given me a particular strain of motivation, one of the bittersweet parts of such traumatic loss, so I latched on to that motivation and felt strength in that.

I had passed the one-year mark and felt the full force of the trauma. It was like someone had taken me by the shoulders and twisted me around, forcing me to face it, relive it and feel the full impact of it again. By accepting the impact, not the loss of Jock, I felt I had been released from the depths of grief somehow. I understand the theory of acceptance being one of Elisabeth Kübler-Ross's five stages of grief; my version was accepting the impact and aftermath. I can never see myself accepting that Jock is gone. I'm not denying it; my mind and heart simply can't accept it to be true. I hold him with me every day, so it doesn't feel like he's truly gone. Having felt the impact and

then the contrast of the release, I knew the trip back to Italy was the right decision. In my meditation, I manifested the feeling of being on that trip. I didn't see anything; I didn't replay moments from previous trips there with Jock. I manifested a feeling, and it was one of calmness and gratitude at the sheer beauty of seeing the sun rise or set over the horizon. It was this image that I kept taking my mind to if I got scared of going, or if I woke in the night and started having negative thoughts; I took deep breaths and let my mind go back to that feeling.

Italy. Again.

I woke the kids at 4.30 am, and our little family headed off on what I was hoping would be our ultimate adventure. I had asked myself if it was too risky – *Am I removing all stability, consistency and habit for the kids?* Was I taking them away from the friends and family who have been so critical in their recovery, from the place where their new seeds have been sown, and possibly making them even more confused about where 'home' was? Both kids were already confused between Melbourne, Sydney and Rome. Alfie had said to me a few months earlier that he liked our hotel. I asked what he meant, and he said the house we had borrowed from a friend. He was actually referring to the house that we were living in and paying rent on. He had become so accustomed to everyone stepping in and

looking after us he figured that was what was happening with our house.

It made me sad to think he didn't feel like it was our new home. I had become really attached to it – our first home, just the three of us. It was the smallest house I'd ever had, but it represented a piece of healing, and our house of mourning had been transformed through effort, love and intention. I knew the location next to the ocean had been a critical part of my healing. I loved starting and finishing my day by watching nature do her thing and seeing the weather roll in and out. It confirmed that the universe decides and that very little is under my control, and reminds me to let the current of life drag me forward.

When I spoke to the kids about enjoying an extended holiday back in Italy, Alfie asked if we could go to Singapore as well. He loves it there because on our last family holiday, Jock played with the kids in the pool nonstop, from breakfast through to dinnertime. Jock and I celebrated his last birthday in Singapore. We had dinner at Burnt Ends then went to a million bars and drank Vespers for the rest of the night. It was such a fun night and one of his favourite meals – easily the best birthday celebration that we'd had together.

Alfie wanted to stay at the same hotel in Singapore; I told him I would try. That was a lie – I didn't want to stay there. I set about researching the best kids' hotels in Singapore because I wanted them to have an absolute ball.

I found two that fit my budget and looked really fun; I also looked up our usual hotel. All the prices were about the same, and I could feel Jock telling me to stop wasting my time researching and just book our usual hotel. I couldn't do it, so I put booking the Singapore hotel onto my list of things to do later. Then I thought about it a lot. I imagined walking into the usual hotel and being in the pool with the kids, and I couldn't work out how I would feel. Months passed, and I really needed to get onto the hotel booking. When I looked up the ones I had shortlisted they had both increased their rates substantially, so I looked at our usual hotel and not only was the price the same but they had an offer on with lots of extras, the best being free-flow champagne and cocktails in the bar from midday to 10 pm and a $200 spa voucher. I laughed out loud and smiled, thinking this was Jock's way of forcing my hand: he knew the exact things that would push me across the line.

The whole trip back to Italy was a huge trigger on a highly emotional gun. Jock and I had done this trip together since the year we met, and each year we did it slightly better. We had spent a couple of months in Italy the summer before he died, travelling along the Amalfi Coast, which we had done together every year. Then we travelled around the whole of the Sicilian coast for a month, with some friends joining us for a couple of weeks, before ending in Puglia for a week. Jock was at his happiest in the markets and at the fishmongers in Italy. The pinnacle was when Jock caught

the fish himself, quickly pickled some ginger, then served us sashimi moments later. This was his happy place.

Now, we were going back to revisit these places and these moments, but without him.

I didn't know how hard this would be to conquer. I knew I was in a much better starting position than when we had returned to the Dolomites. Still, starting in Singapore was more of a challenge than I thought it would be. With my self-pledge to try not to cry in front of the kids, I walked past the pool for the first time by myself to practise, and felt a pang. Then, a few hours later, I sat next to it while our little ones played, and I was okay, with no tears. But over the days we stayed there, I watched other dads with their kids in the pool and said aloud, 'I'm sorry, darling.' This would have been the one thing Jock would have done with the kids every day for their whole childhood and continued on with their little ones when he was a nonno.

Alfie wanted me to be the replacement Papa and kept asking me why I wasn't staying in the pool to play with them. I said I wasn't feeling well. I could play with the kids in the pool, but I'd be nowhere near as fun or strong as Jock; nor did I have the endurance or attention span for hours in the pool. It would just be disappointing for the kids. I have attempted to replace so much of Jock, and I am now learning that I can't do that anymore. If I genuinely don't think I will do it well, I explain to the kids that it was a Papa thing, and they accept that now.

I've found that when the kids feel they need to convince me of something or if they are angry at me and want to lash out, they compare me to Jock. For Alfie, it's that I'm slow in the kitchen, I cut the pancetta too thick, or the froth on his coffee milk isn't big like Papa's. Isla uses guilt to get her point across: I ask her to put her seatbelt on herself, and she says Papa always put it on for her; or I ask her to finish her dinner, and she says Papa would never tell her to do that; or when I get angry, she says it makes her sad and that she misses Papa. In fairness, Jock did always put her seatbelt on, and if I ever said the kids had to finish their dinner so they could get gelato, Jock would eat huge mouthfuls of their food while I wasn't looking to make sure they got their gelato. And when Isla cries for any reason now, because her sadness tank is open, she also cries out for Papa. At first it upset me when they would lash out at me like this, but it doesn't affect me now, and I'm not angry at them for doing it. I wish they'd stop, but I figure they'll get there in their own time, kind of like the cutlery thing.

We had five days in Singapore on the way to Italy. On the third day, I received an email from the real estate agent we had rented a place from on the Amalfi Coast, saying that they had 'accidentally' booked three other reservations over the top of ours. We could stay the first ten days but then we needed to find alternative accommodation. I had booked 80 days at this place and imagined we

would settle in and feel local. I had organised an Italian tutor for the kids, and I really thought I had nailed this arrangement. Obviously, the Italians had a different plan for me.

When we arrived at the rental property, the boss of the real estate agency was there as well as the person I had been dealing with over email to make the booking. The boss only spoke Italian, and he was screaming at me, arms waving, trying to tower over me and threaten me. I showed him the emails with the confirmation details, negotiated rate and deposit receipt, which made him even angrier. He was yelling at the other guy, then back at me, and my kids were standing there watching this unfold. Finally, I told the guy I had been dealing with, who spoke English, that if his boss didn't stop yelling and threatening me in front of my children I was going to call the police. He repeated what I had said, and the boss stopped yelling at me. Then I told him that if my husband were here, he wouldn't be speaking to me like this, and would instead have copped a couple of Glasgow kisses to his face. I have had a few of these moments when I've gotten a solid reminder that Jock isn't here to protect me or defend me anymore. I also know that I am treated differently as a single woman than when I was with Jock. In this instance, I felt physically threatened, and I didn't want my little ones to witness me being abused like this by a man. The angry man stopped, and I asked the other guy if he could make sure his boss

didn't return to the property while I was renting it, and he said he would take care of it.

That night, I sat out on the verandah with the kids, watching the sun set over the horizon, and I decided Italy was not the place for me to raise our children. Italy was a place I adored, and we would be spending our holidays there whenever possible, but it didn't give me the security or predictability I needed now. The way I had been treated by the landlord and the school principal in Rome in the couple of weeks after losing Jock was disgraceful, and now this. It was the universe telling me to let that dream float away and to stop willing it to be. The clarity of that decision gave me an unexpected release, and I was grateful that the question of us living there had been so clearly answered in my mind.

On one of our first nights there, I went out for Solo Date Night to have some time to work on this book. As I walked home on a spectacular balmy summer's night, I was hit by how much I missed Jock. I sat down and cried, the kind where I wondered if I was going to vomit. I missed him so much that it physically stopped me in my tracks. This was a part of the world I had only ever been to with Jock; it was our adventure, where we fell more and more in love with each other and with Italy, and now I was here writing a book on grief and traumatic loss. How did I get dealt these cards? Were they given to me because I deserved this level of pain? Or because someone had to live through this, and

the universe decided it was going to be me? I pulled myself together and walked the last street home.

As I got closer, I could hear our little ones on the terrace of our apartment. They were laughing their asses off; I could hear Isla yelling out to Alfie to stop being cheeky before they both laughed uncontrollably again. Hearing that soundtrack in that moment broke my heart all over again. By the time I felt capable of walking in the door, I had calmed down, but when the kids ran to cuddle me, Alfie cradled my face and asked what was wrong, why I had been crying. Isla told him knowingly that Papa made me cry. I put my arms around both of them and sobbed uncontrollably into them. They hugged me back, not releasing their hold until I did. I went and had a shower, angry at myself for crying in front of them and using their cuddles as my nurture. This had to stop.

During the first week of our trip, I spent a few days hanging with some friends from Australia who were also travelling on the Amalfi Coast. I met them at Da Adolfo, a restaurant that Jock and I loved going to together. One of the photos I have in my bedroom now is of our first lunch there together. It was a big emotional hurdle to walk into that restaurant. I travelled there alone – the others were coming as a group – and arrived early to acclimatise myself. I had an Americano, and sat looking at the view that Jock and I had looked at together so many times. We never ate there with anyone; it was always just the two

of us. I had about half an hour until everyone arrived, so I went for a swim.

As I floated on my back in the water and looked up at the rocks, I asked myself if I would have been better off never having met Jock. If never having to live through these feelings was better than having had my eight years with him. I have asked myself that question a few times. I have also asked myself if the kids would have been better off if I had died and he had lived. Each time, my mind flicks to our little ones, and I know these hypotheticals can never be answered. They are my purpose now, and I had never felt more like their mamma than I did in this moment. I felt empowered bringing them to the other side of the world, by surviving the last eighteen months, and to be back floating in the Mediterranean where I had floated with Jock, able to say to myself that I really was okay and in a happy place.

I had told Macca, one of my close friends who was coming with the group to lunch, that this would be a triggering location for me. When he arrived, he gave me an enormous hug, took his sunglasses off and looked at me, and asked if I was okay. He said that if anything changed, he was there for me. I told him absolutely, and we released then got on with our lunch. I think there are two camps of grief huggers – those who trust when you say you're okay, and let go and carry on, and those who overstay their hug either because they're not okay or they want you to cry on their shoulder so they have a purpose.

The next day, we all took a boat tour around Capri and the beautiful Faraglioni rock formations. The middle one has an archway that you drive the boat through, and legend has it that the lover that you kiss as you go through the archway is the one you will have everlasting love and fertility with. Jock and I went through there together on our first trip to Capri and kissed as we went through. Now, as we were all preparing to go through the archway, I was sitting off by myself, and Macca asked if I wanted to move and sit with them. I said I was okay and he respected that. As we approached the archway, I had my second cry of the trip. My eternal lover was Jock, and I wanted to go back in time and have this moment with him again. I don't want to go through the archway with anyone; I had done that and committed to a life with Jock, and as we sailed around the rest of the afternoon, I wondered if it was possible to ever truly love someone again. I always felt my love for Jock physically. Any time we hugged I felt a pang; I felt better with his closeness.

I finished my fun few days with these friends and returned to my little family. I had really missed them; after lunch at Da Adolfo on the first day, I had just wanted to go home to them and be on our adventure together. Mum guilt was at an all-time high, and I also just missed their touch.

After I returned we moved out of the angry Italian's place and into Monica's house. She was a gorgeous Mexican woman who had lived in Italy for a couple of decades. Her

house had a goat, chickens, dogs, cats – the kids were in wonderland, me not so much. Monica would drop by with something from her enormous terraced garden each day – almonds, figs, tomatoes, basil. She had looked at my Instagram account and worked out that Jock was my husband, so had driven to Cetara to buy me a bottle of colatura di alici because that was one of the last videos I had posted on Jock's socials. She would bring the goat up to our front door so the kids could feed it milk from a bottle; she helped me carry our suitcases up the 60 stairs to the road when it was time to go. The universe gifted me Monica: not only did she save my skin by having a place available for a long period of time and within my budget, but she also showed me the joy and frustration of living in Italy when you're not an Italian. It was good confirmation of my sunset decision to visit but not live in Italy.

We would spend each day down by the ocean. The kids practised swimming all day, and day by day, they improved dramatically. That meant I could sit nearby, reading my book, and not be worried that if either of them fell in, they may not come back up. Now, they were lying down on the pebbles where the waves were crashing so they'd get thrown around. They thought this was hilarious. Months before, if that had happened at the beach, Alfie would have been hysterical and insisted we go home. The kids were thriving in Italy: it was familiar, they weren't shy and they felt freedom being on our little adventure.

On 4 August it was Jock's birthday, so the kids and I went to Da Adolfo together for lunch. We swam, ate, swam again, and I just wanted Jock to see this. His little family was in a remote spot on the Amalfi Coast celebrating him. I wasn't sad this birthday; I knew he was happy that I had chosen this place for the three of us to celebrate. I held the kids close all day, both of them on me or against me the whole time.

Another special time on this trip was when Ava and Johnny came to visit us for a week. I realised that was exactly what I needed – Ava is always so easy to hang out with, and so that's what we did. And Johnny brings a Jock-like energy.

I felt an anonymity living in a small village in Italy, and thought we might be able to stay in that bubble for the whole time we were there. But that wasn't to be. One day at a restaurant, a waiter came up to me and told me how much he loved Jock, that he was his favourite *MasterChef* judge. He was speaking about Jock like he was still alive, which made it even more awkward. I was polite and wrapped up the conversation as soon as I could. Another day, I was swimming with the kids, and a woman came over to tell me she was a big fan of Jock's and that I was doing a great job. She had two young kids the same age as Alfie and Isla, and had been watching me swim and play with them – she said she had no idea how I would have been able to keep parenting

after such a huge loss. I thanked her, then let the kids distract me and drag me away.

I had been going to the gym a lot before we went away as I wanted to be as strong and healthy as possible on this holiday. There was one gym in the Amalfi Coast, which we lived behind, so I went there most days. It was truly dysfunctional. The hand weights had different weights on each end, the fabric on the equipment was so torn it cut into your skin and the weights didn't fit onto the end of the dumbbells. I took the kids with me, and I let them use their iPads – we have a rule that they can't be used outside of the house – so they loved going to the gym. It was during one of these visits that I had an unexpectedly important moment, when Isla asked why I was at the gym. I told her it was because I wanted to be strong, and it kept me healthy. She asked again, why, and I said that now that we didn't have Papa around, I had to do more of the Papa things, and that was hard for me. She didn't use her iPad that day; she just watched me working out. She copied some of my movements, and when I was getting to the end of a set and she could see I was struggling, she would shout out, 'Go, Mamma! Go, Mamma!' When we left that day, she told me that gelato makes you fat. I stopped in my tracks. I said that wasn't true, that we eat everything in moderation and being strong was more important than not being fat. We walked on, me shaking my head that I had to have a conversation about body image with a three-year-old girl.

The kids moved through the trip as my ultimate travel buddies. We had agreed they would try at least one new food daily. No problem. Before too long Isla was ordering anchovies for her entree, they were eating vongole quicker than any human ever had, they were filleting their own barbecue sardines, adding a squeeze of lemon and reaching for the next one. These food moments made me really proud of them, but also proud that I had been able to maintain something that was so important to Jock. He had the kids eating our food as soon as possible, even if he had to blend it for them. He had them adding pepper and chilli to their food way too early, and now they continued doing that. As they ate new foods I taught them the Italian words – alice, prosciutto cotto, fiche, formaggio – which they would repeat for me once, and that would be how they referred to the food from that moment on.

As the trip passed us by, the kids just kept growing. I had bought them new shoes before we left, and now their toes were hanging out the front of their sandals. I bought new, larger shoes, and by the time we returned to Australia, they had grown out of them too. They also grew out of maybe 50 per cent of their clothes, so I donated them before we flew home. The sun and healthy food agreed with them, and it made me happy that they were doing some of their growing up in Italy.

First Wave

The first wave of loss passed; it was a big one, and we moved through it. Jock and I used to say we were stronger together than apart. I saw us as two mountains out in the wilderness, getting along just fine as individuals. But when we came together, we created a valley, and in that valley, everything prospered. Rivers flowed, things grew and we created something together that wasn't possible apart. I see myself and the three kids the same way – we weathered the first wave together. There was no getting around it; moving through it was the only way to let the wave pass. We went through it at different paces, with different awareness, with different losses, but shoulder to shoulder the whole way. We have coped in very different ways, but I know we're all safely on the other side of it now.

I also acknowledge that I experienced a version of affluent mourning. I know I made it through this first wave from a place of privilege and support. I had money in the bank, I could afford a babysitter, I didn't have the demands of a full-time job or an employer. I also had the support of anyone in the world that I needed support from. And I mean that in all seriousness. I called on people in every corner of the world for favours big and small, and every time they answered my call and went over and above for me. I know this is not the path for many people, and I think it was the universe apologising to us for having to grieve so publicly. There was an imbalance in the empathy people felt for me and continue to feel for me, and I appreciate it so much, but I know others haven't had that gift.

The next wave is somewhere in the distance; it's far from smooth waters from here on, but it won't be like that first one. I am so profoundly proud of the kids, I am proud of myself and I am proud of our little family unit. We have all instinctively acted with our heart first and mind second, which has meant we are navigating this authentically. Not all conversations have been rosy, and not all learnings have been insightful, but we are a family with the heart ripped out of it, and it has taken some work to get our pulse back to the right cadence.

The children have started having conversations with each other and with me about heaven. It's a concept I didn't introduce them to, so I am uncertain where it

came from. It makes sense to them, and they're not asking tricky questions that I don't know the answers to, but I am sure they will. A friend of ours lost one of their dogs, and Alfie explained to Isla that Hugo was now up in heaven with Papa, so he was okay. He said that anyone who dies goes to Papa. Alfie saw Jock as a person who looked after everyone as he looked after us, and I loved hearing his little brain compute what heaven and an afterlife looked like. It was obvious to him that his Papa was the heart of that place too.

Our children have weaved loss and death into their daily lives. Not one day goes by where they don't speak about Jock, to me or to each other. On the weekend, they were playing in the park, and another kid's dad couldn't see where Alfie and Isla's parents were as I was sitting on a bench watching, so he asked Isla, 'Where's your mum and dad?' She said, 'Mamma is over there. Papa is dead, and he's in the grass.' The man came over to speak to me and share his condolences; he also apologised for making that assumption and forcing Isla to say those words. It was totally unnecessary: Jock and death are not taboo in our home. Today, as I was dropping the kids off at school and daycare, Alfie said something I couldn't hear so I asked if he could speak up. He told me it was okay, he was just speaking to Papa. Sure, this may be of concern at some point in his life, but for now, it gives us all comfort, and I'm okay with it.

I wouldn't say Jock and I had a thorough plan for life, but I can say this certainly was not anywhere on my radar. I am now at peace with handing myself over to it. I know that the universe can only drag me forward – that's the beauty of being more spiritual now, because as I look forward, I move forward. I have grown increasingly impatient with sadness, with grief and with thinking I was healed in places and then finding out I wasn't. But I get strength from knowing I am not gliding through life and that I am moving with intention. I imagine myself walking through life now, and it's not just walking with one foot in front of the other. It feels like I am making small jumps from one stepping stone to the next, keeping my eyes wide open and looking forward so I can move safely. Each small jump is considered and weighed up, and then I go for it. I refuse to be a passenger in life, shuffling forward without ever needing to take leaps of faith. I have been gifted this one life and want to live every part of it.

I also take being Ava, Alfie and Isla's mamma more seriously than ever. I value my health; I need to be strong, I need to be safe and I need to show them I am emotionally and physically there to support them. My mental health has peaked and dropped, and finding a consistent balance is a daily task. Some days, I am proud of myself; others, I'm appalled. I know that when my mind takes me to places of sadness or anger at Jock for leaving me in this

alone, I can't sit in that mindset and also parent our little ones fairly. I know that when I have a few wines with Ava and then talk about Jock nonstop, that isn't helping her. And I am very aware that night-time grief is no longer welcome in my life.

This doesn't mean I am blocking any emotions or feelings; I simply am at a point where I need to exercise some control. I cannot break open whenever I feel like it. Everyone is walking through their days with shit going on, but they're all functioning most of the time. Putting some discipline in place has helped stop my excuse-making. I was given a lot of freedom to figure myself out, sleep until the kids woke me up, take them on holidays and work in the moments I felt I could do a good job. But now, I need discipline and habits.

I returned from our Italian adventure and fell straight into this new version of myself, Lauren 3.0, coined by one of my friends. It's not a brand-new version; it's not a kintsugi version of the previous versions of me. She is a strong woman and mother with a different sense of strength and capability. Living this version of me means doing hard things, asking for help and leaning on others with no need for thanks or regret. This version of me enjoys working hard and achieving because it provides for our family. Everything starts and ends with me and, instead of over-whelming me like it has in the past, this knowledge powers me on and pushes me further.

I crave the simplest of moments, like those we had in Italy, the kids' laughter in the night air. I know that I have worked hard to get us here, and I can now relax and enjoy these moments without sadness and tears. I am blessed to have so many instances of gratitude and bliss in front of me every day because I have Jock's three children in my world. They are my world.

Just before we left for our Italian adventure, I felt we had turned a corner. That no matter what the current of life did, we couldn't be dragged back. But only Italy could confirm that and tell me I was truly okay, and let me do this pressure testing. And it gave me the very clear answer that I had, in fact, conquered the first wave – I hadn't survived it or dragged myself through to the finish line. I had pushed through it and emerged as this different version of myself, a woman I recognised and enjoyed being, and one who had been defined by Jock's death.

Apparently, to get through the first wave of grief means you have worked through the five stages of mourning – denial, anger, bargaining, depression and acceptance. I have been more thorough with some of those stages than others. I have used the information I could gather, and that has anchored me; otherwise, I would still be adrift and feel the helplessness I felt in the first months after losing Jock. But I truly don't see how I will ever accept losing Jock. What I can accept is that I have responsibilities that should have been shared with Jock but are now solely mine. I accept that

our children don't have a papa who is physically present for them. And I accept the impact of the heart being ripped out of our family.

Jock chose the woman who deeply understood him, understood trauma and addiction, and loved him beyond possibility. He chose the right woman to marry in me. And he chose the right mamma for his children. I find strength in knowing, without question, that Jock made the right decisions. I am the person to get our little family, and our friends and extended family, through this. I have emerged stronger and more capable than I ever thought possible, maybe something Jock intuitively knew. I have been authentic and true throughout the process, and that is the secret I am now privy to. I wanted to find a modest way of saying this, but I can't. I was chosen by Jock and I'm now the one left standing.

Till Death Do Us Part

The words 'till death do us part' make sense; some have said them in their wedding vows. But they're not true words to me now that I have lived them.

Death made us. Death gave me Jock forever. Death defined who I am and the person and mother I needed to become. We will never be apart. I will be buried with Jock; we will be together eternally, at peace in the shadow of his eucalyptus trees and beloved kookaburras. I will live a long life, and when I join him, it will be time; the kids will not have their other parent taken from them so unfairly. Jock and I will live on in them forever, and I will have taught them every part of their papa, including the parts he didn't even see in himself.

My spirituality has come from not believing that death takes someone away. I cannot get my head to comprehend

that Jock could have lived on earth, having impact every day, and then just not be here anymore. The memory of Jock lives on in so many, and that memory keeps him here. Maybe one day, there will be no one left on earth who knows him or has been impacted by him, and then perhaps I could understand the concept of someone dying and disappearing. For many people, I represent Jock now. So, instead of us parting, we are more one now than ever.

Jock and I were pretty much the male and female version of each other, but he always wanted to surround everything with fun and cheekiness. His appetite for lifting people up, for genuinely and deeply caring, did not come naturally to me. I could do it for my dearest friends, but that was it. Jock would do it for anyone who even hinted at a need. It annoyed me; it felt like he was endlessly distracted by people who needed his care or attention. Then we lost him, and this was one of his traits that I admired the most. I have many moments of being angry at myself for not supporting him in this need of his. I think there was a well he wanted to fill, and I wish I had been more supportive and accepting of that.

In saying that, I was supportive in every other part of his life. His children, his work, his childhood trauma. Whatever he needed, even if he didn't realise it, I was there to prop him up. I was a good wife. In my lowest, most silent moments, I say that to myself. Loyal beyond words

or actions, then and always. I have rewritten my wedding vows to Jock since he died. They were filled with hope for our life together, growing old together, and making a life that was the exact one we were meant to be living. My vows now are filled with a love and admiration that can never be broken, that even without any effort, grow constantly. He is my person, he is my husband, he is the love of my life, he is the one I was meant to be bound to. But now that we are not physically able to be married, I need freedom to reinvent myself and find new happiness.

Like most of the people walking the earth, I have grief as a powerful part of my emotional repertoire. Grief is part of my life; I am now not afraid of when it might strike or show itself. I know how to get it under control, how to let it roam free in my mind or my words, and when that is appropriate or too much. Jock's life and livelihood were broken time and time again, and he kept having the courage to pick up the pieces, stick them back together and keep moving. He collected meaning from these rebuilds; he proved to himself that he was stronger and more capable than the trauma that tried to drown out the good parts of him. He craved understanding and forgiveness; he craved simple happiness and moments of joy. I know this of my gorgeous husband, and I continue to give him these things even in death and the constant silence of loss.

My love for Jock is out of my control – he gave me no choice but to fall madly, deeply in love with him from the

first moment I was in his presence. I feel a love-sickness for him that I sense physically at times, the ache of loving him and wanting to touch him like we were meeting again. Oh, to meet Jock just one more time. To have just one more moment with him. I wouldn't even need to say any words or to touch him; it's one of the bargains I have tried to make with the universe when I feel weak or missing him becomes too unbearable. It's the simplest of fantasies, but will never be again.

I feed off hope – my energy comes from believing that life is meant to be beautiful and will be if you just let it. I have moments of excessive doubt; I let the negative thoughts play over and over in my mind, and most of the time, I have the power to shut them down and let them float away so they're out of reach. When these moments knock me over, I get up faster now. I know it's just a temporary loss of balance in my world. I know the power of falling in love, of being in love, and the reliance on it.

There will be a piece missing from me for the rest of my life; losing Jock has been the greatest robbery. That gives me the belief, possibly faith, that everything else around me will grow back even healthier than before. In some moments of doubt, I feel like I am a victim that has been dealt an unfair blow to a life being really well lived. When I first lost Jock, every day felt drained of colour. But one by one, the days have become colourful again, and I feel happy that I am no longer colour-blind. I have felt guilt,

I have felt like I am not being the wife Jock deserves, or that I'm not memorialising Jock enough for the kids – then I realise that just isn't true. I have used the time since Jock died as a stage to analyse my life, and look at ways to do it even better this time. The metaphor I have painted for myself is that I have been looking through a magnifying glass, staying focused, and now I can start lighting fires again in my life.

Till death do us part is only the beginning of my love and loyalty to the gorgeous man who was my husband. My love. My greatest loss. I carry him with me always.

Resources

Griefline
Support for anyone experiencing grief
griefline.org.au
1300 845 745

Grief Australia
Grief support, counselling and education
grief.org.au
+61 3 9265 2100

National Centre for Childhood Grief
Not-for-profit organisation dedicated to caring for bereaved
children and their families following the death of a parent,
sibling or other close loved one
childhoodgrief.org.au
1300 654 556

Parent Line
Free telephone counselling and support service for parents
and carers of children aged 0 to 18 in New South Wales
parentline.org.au
1300 1300 52

Jock's Carbonara Recipe

So many of Jock's stories from his childhood were about his nonno, who he adored but sadly lost when he was only a boy. Nonno's sense of style, his personality and his cooking ability were all things Jock admired and aspired to have when he grew up.

Carbonara became the dish that Jock perfected – he would make it for us at home, when friends dropped in unexpectedly, or if we were travelling around the world and he could get his hands on a good piece of guanciale.

When Isla started to eat solids, this was her first meal. Jock sat her on the bench and spooned it into her mouth. Most parents start with rice, cereal or mashed vegetables – not in our house!

Spaghetti Carbonara

INGREDIENTS – Serves 2
250 g spaghetti (dried pasta is totally fine!)
80 g guanciale, diced
1 egg
3 egg yolks
60 g pecorino romano
60 g parmigiano reggiano
pasta water
salt and pepper

METHOD
Bring a pot of water to a boil and add a pinch of salt, then cook pasta.

Meanwhile, in a large skillet, add the guanciale and cook over medium-high heat, stirring frequently until the guanciale is golden brown. This will take up to 5 minutes. Then remove and strain the guanciale, catching all of the fat in a bowl. Put the guanciale to the side and add the strained fat back into the pan, over a very low heat.

In a large bowl, whisk together the egg, yolks and cheese.

Once the pasta is cooked, strain it in a colander, catching a mug full of pasta water to use for the sauce. Add the

cooked pasta to the pan with the cooked guanciale and the fat and stir through until the pasta is completely coated.

Next, add about half the mug of pasta water into the egg/cheese mix and whisk well. Pour the egg/cheese mix into the pasta pan and ensure the heat is on the lowest setting. Gently toss the pasta in the sauce until it begins to thicken (3–4 minutes), then remove from the heat, adjust the seasoning, place a clean tea towel over the bowl and let the pasta rest for 4 minutes. Remove the tea towel, adjust the consistency using the pasta water, and serve immediately.

Powered by Penguin

Looking for more great reads, exclusive content and book giveaways?

Subscribe to our weekly newsletter.

Scan the QR code or visit penguin.com.au/signup

Printed in Great Britain
by Amazon